D0079462

The Career Arts

The
Career Arts

Making the Most
of College, Credentials,
and Connections

Ben Wildavsky

PRINCETON UNIVERSITY PRESS

PRINCETON & OXFORD

Published by Princeton University Press
41 William Street, Princeton, New Jersey 08540
99 Banbury Road, Oxford OX2 6JX

press.princeton.edu

All Rights Reserved

Library of Congress Cataloging-in-Publication Data

Names: Wildavsky, Ben, author.
Title: The career arts : making the most of college, credentials, and
    connections / Ben Wildavsky.
Description: Princeton : Princeton University Press, [2023] |
    Includes bibliographical references and index.
Identifiers: LCCN 2023003328 (print) | LCCN 2023003329 (ebook) |
    ISBN 9780691239798 (hardback) | ISBN 9780691239804 (ebook)
Subjects: LCSH: Student aspirations. | School-to-work transition. |
    Career development. | College preparation programs. | College student
    orientation. | High school graduates—Life skills guides. | Vocational guidance. |
    BISAC: EDUCATION / Schools / Levels / Higher | EDUCATION / History
Classification: LCC LB1027.8 .W55 2024 (print) | LCC LB1027.8 (ebook) |
    DDC 331.702/33—dc23/eng/20230426
LC record available at https://lccn.loc.gov/2023003328
LC ebook record available at https://lccn.loc.gov/2023003329

British Library Cataloging-in-Publication Data is available

Editorial: Peter Dougherty, Matt Rohal, and Alena Chekanov
Production Editorial: Ali Parrington
Text Design: Karl Spurzem
Jacket Design: Katie Osborne
Production: Erin Suydam
Publicity: Maria Whelan and Kathryn Stevens
Copyeditor: Kathleen Kageff

This book has been composed in Arno Pro with Firelli Variable

Printed on acid-free paper. ∞

Printed in the United States of America

10 9 8 7 6 5 4 3 2 1

For Rachel

Contents

Acknowledgments

My effort to write a short, accessible book on education and careers rested on the thoughtful input and strong backing of a remarkably long list of people and institutions. When I step back and look at the themes I've explored here, I see a direct connection between the evolution of my thinking and my career as a journalist and at the Kauffman Foundation, the Brookings Institution, the State University of New York's Rockefeller Institute of Government, the College Board, Strada Education Network, and the University of Virginia. I'm grateful to the leaders of those organizations and others who made it possible for me to learn by writing, speaking, convening, teaching, researching, and interviewing leading education and workforce thinkers.

My time at Strada was particularly helpful in exposing me to different schools of thought about broad and targeted education and training, plus the value of social capital. I learned a lot by launching and hosting Strada's *Lessons Earned* podcast, with valued cohosts who included Andrew Hanson and Aimée Eubanks Davis, and later by starting up my new *Higher Ed Spotlight* podcast. Guests from both shows are quoted in this book.

I began exploring the connection between education, careers, and economic mobility much earlier, including as a book reviewer, conference organizer, consultant, and blogger for the *Chronicle of Higher Education* and Education Sector. More recently, I honed my thinking by speaking and moderating panel discussions at the Arizona State University REMOTE Connected Faculty Summit, Minnesota State College Southeast, Monash University, P3•EDU at the University of Colorado Denver, and at my current institutional home, the University of Virginia School of Education and Human Development.

At UVA, I'm grateful to former dean Bob Pianta for making possible my visiting scholar appointment, to current dean Stephanie Rowley, to colleagues Allison Atteberry, Ben Castleman, Shannon Kontalonis, Beth Schueler, Sarah Turner, and Jim Wyckoff, and to the PhD students who attended my work-in-progress presentation and offered useful questions and suggestions (including one that led me to consider making a TikTok video to highlight my recommendations for students who may not wish to read an entire book). I've been fortunate to make use of UVA's great library, with help from its efficient librarians, and to have access to well-appointed office space in Arlington, Virginia.

I owe special thanks to longtime Princeton University Press director and editor at large Peter Dougherty. In the best tradition of visionary editors, Peter was a valued partner in conceiving and shaping this book. He and I had discussed an earlier version of my idea a few years ago. When I wanted to tackle it again with a revised approach, he was instrumental in helping me craft my early concept into a successful proposal that closely tracks the final form of the book. At every step of the way he has offered unflagging encouragement and a steady stream of great ideas.

On Peter's retirement from PUP, he passed the baton to another talented editor, Matt Rohal, who has done a superb job bringing the book to the finish line. My thanks to Peter, Matt, and many others at PUP, including Ginny Armenti, Sydney Bartlett, David Campbell, Alena Chekanov, Debbie Greco, Kathleen Kageff, Scot Kuehm, Ali Parrington, and Maria Whelan. I'm also grateful to the outside readers who reviewed the manuscript, recommended publication, and offered many helpful suggestions.

The Smith Richardson Foundation and the Bill & Melinda Gates Foundation provided invaluable grant support for this book. At Smith Richardson, program officer Mark Steinmeyer made many important substantive suggestions about relevant research that improved the final manuscript. My work also benefited from Julia Paolillo's excellent research assistance. She brought to the project careful attention to detail, strong background knowledge, and welcome enthusiasm. On the way to publication, Elyse Ashburn and Paul Fain at *Work Shift*, and Gary Rosen at the *Wall Street Journal*, gave me important opportunities to road test my ideas by publishing early articles drawn from my work-in-progress.

I am grateful to all those whose ideas and analysis I quote and cite in these pages. The following individuals, whether mentioned by name in the book or not, were especially generous with their time and insights, from providing background reading and source ideas, to reviewing the manuscript, to offering introductions, practical assistance, and encouragement: Tony Carnevale,

Tom Dawson, David Deming, Sue Dynarski, Aimée Eubanks Davis, Checker Finn, Julia Freeland Fisher, Sean Gallagher, Andrew Hanson, Carrie Besnette Hauser, Michael Horn, Meghan Hughes, Bill Jackson, Tom Kane, Larry Katz, Martin Kurzweil, Bob Lerman, Rachel Lipson, Bob Litan, Dewayne Mathews, Brent Orrell, Matt Sigelman, Mitchell Stevens, John Thelin, Judy Wade, Garrett Warfield, and Martin West. Any mistakes or analytical missteps are entirely my own. Or, as my late father once wrote in a similar context, I alone am irresponsible.

As I worked on *The Career Arts*, it was a pleasure to watch my children, Eva, Aaron, and Saul, and my daughter-in-law, Deena, continue their own promising educational and career journeys. I also had the good fortune, as I have for more than thirty years, to benefit from the immense good sense, expert editorial feedback, and loving support of my wife, Rachel. This book is dedicated to her.

The Career Arts

Chapter 1

Answering the Big Questions about College and Career

In the past century, Americans have widely embraced the promise of postsecondary education. They've seen college, in all its varied forms, as a vital pathway to upward mobility. But in recent years they have become considerably less certain and more anxious about its career value.

On the one hand, the percentage of recent high school completers enrolling in college rose from 51 percent in 1970 to 69 percent in 2018, fueled by frequently cited income and job benefits for degree holders. By 2021, the percentage of Americans with a bachelor's degree or higher was at an all-time high.[1] On the other, nearly half of US parents now say they want alternatives to four-year college for their children, according to a Gallup poll released in April 2021. That's about evenly split with the 54 percent who still want their high school graduates to attend college. And it continues an extraordinary trend that saw the percentage of Americans who call a college education "very important" fall from 70 percent to 51 percent in just *six years* from 2013 to 2019.[2]

The disruption of the global Covid-19 pandemic, combined with preexisting concerns about college value, only served to accelerate this trajectory. By the spring of 2022, two years into the pandemic, headlines proclaimed a massive drop in US college enrollment. Undergraduate enrollment had dropped by about 1.4 million since the pandemic began, with particularly sharp declines in community colleges and public four-year institutions.[3] This massive decline comes on top of new data showing a record number of Americans—thirty-nine million, according to the National Student Clearinghouse—who have completed some college without earning a degree. With tuition and student debt rising steeply, many have ended up with the worst of both worlds—debt but no degree.

Why the lack of public confidence in college? And why the poor record of persistence to graduation for so many students? Even as policy makers debate tuition-free community college and broad student debt reduction, skeptics raise fundamental questions about whether the apparent benefits of higher education are real. Are we certain that college provides a path to employment that reliably ensures return on investment? Does the marketplace value of degrees rest more on signaling—the so-called sheepskin effect—than on real, career-enhancing learning? And are too many Americans being pushed to go to college, only to fail to complete it, or to graduate into underemployment and crippling debt at a time when the college wage premium is no longer rising?

Behind these questions lies what many see as a central trade-off between pure academics and more practical, job-relevant skills. Amid rising costs and growing student debt, that dichotomy has taken on greater urgency. Do we need philosophers or welders? During an economic recovery or job transition, is coding boot camp or a targeted, job-specific credential a better bet than a BA? The stakes are high for young learners, midcareer workers, and those seeking to give them the best opportunities in life.

This book will explore these questions and offer readers some answers in chapters on the value of college degrees, which nondegree alternatives are most useful, and the decisive importance of building social capital to turn education into career success. My narrative will make extensive use of research and data; stories of ordinary people; interviews with experts; and case studies that illustrate effective practices and organizations. The arguments developed in each chapter will build toward the set of eight practices that give this book its name: the career arts.

These eight recommended practices, summarized in the final chapter, range from the continued value of going to college and the need to pursue a combination of broad and targeted skills to the purposeful approach needed to make the best use of nondegree options. *The Career Arts* is aimed at young adults and students of all ages who seek guidelines for getting ahead. The career arts can also shape the efforts of parents, counselors, educators, workforce leaders, and policy makers who want to help more people reach their educational and career goals.

To avoid mission creep, my focus will be the economic advancement that remains the central goal of education and training for most people. Other important outcomes will be mentioned briefly (learning for its own sake, personal satisfaction) or not at all (civic involvement, better health). Nor will the book examine the complex and unfortunate intersection between high-profile campus culture wars and public concern about the economic value of college. My aim is to lay out the evidence, the arguments, and the trade-offs that should be considered by anybody seeking to understand how to get ahead as they make decisions about college, alternative credentials, and building professional networks.

The Real World of Hybrid Studies and Hybrid Jobs

The variety of offerings and competing demands, both broad and focused, facing American higher education are on full display at Colorado Mountain College, a public college with eleven campuses in high-cost mountain resort communities. Colorado Mountain College is one of about four hundred[4] "dual-mission" institutions around the country, which means it offers a mix of undergraduate programs, including bachelor's and associate degrees as well as specialized certificates. Blending some characteristics of a community college with others of a four-year school, it combines the liberal arts with applied career-oriented training. The intentional set of options includes certifications in fields like law enforcement, culinary arts, and avalanche science; associate degrees in majors from English literature to anthropology; and professionally focused bachelor's degrees in high demand for residents who plan to become teachers, nurses, or national forest managers, to cite a few examples. "We're not competing in a big urban marketplace with multiple colleges and universities," says CMC president Carrie Besnette Hauser. "If we don't offer it, local students don't have access to it, and our regional workforce partners don't get the trained employees they need."[5]

While CMC is distinctive in many ways, including how it is financed, the mixture of targeted skills and broad liberal arts it offers reflects the choices available at a wide range of educational institutions—and comes in direct response to the range of applied and broad skills sought by many employers. Whether students come from local communities or have relocated to the Rockies after previous careers and degrees, many are drawn to specialized credentials needed for the thriving outdoor and tourism industries for which the region is so well known.

Yet Hauser points out that the same employers also seek workers with a range of abilities that will make them valuable over the long term. An outdoor guide, for example, should also be able to work with spreadsheets, communicate with clients, help design a website, and market the enterprise. A fly fishing instructor who ultimately wants to own or start a business will need to compete in a crowded marketplace and likely have some understanding of everything from sales to environmental science. That's why CMC aims to ensure its students, who don't always acquire credentials in a straight line from a certificate to an associate degree to a bachelor's, are equipped with a mixture of targeted career and technical education, or CTE, and broader transferable skills.

"We want learners who come out of CMC to know how to think," she says. "We want them to be critically engaged in conversations, in their communities and their disciplines. We want them to know how to write and communicate." In brief, Hauser explains, "we do liberal arts *and* career-focused skills training—and smash them together."

The mixture of skills offered at Colorado Mountain College and other dual-mission institutions, and the reasons Hauser cites for their utility, are strikingly similar to those described by the labor market analytics firm Burning Glass Technologies in a report on the mixture of technical and creative thinking required by a growing number of "hybrid jobs."[6] Drawing on its massive database of hundreds of millions of online job postings, résumés, and social profiles, the firm—now known as Lightcast—documented much faster job growth in positions requiring a mixture of what the *Wall Street Journal* characterized as creative or social "right-brain" jobs supplemented by "left-brain" technical skills. It also showed that hybrid jobs combining, say, advertising and data science skills, pay more than those requiring a more typical or conventional mixture of abilities. A marketing manager who knows the database program SQL, according to the analysis, can earn $100,000 annually on average—41 percent more than the $71,000 earned by a colleague without those skills.[7] What's more, hybrid jobs are less likely to be automated. "The jobs that are growing the fastest, that are of highest value," Burning Glass Institute president Matt Sigelman told me in an interview, "are the ones that are blending skills."[8]

The Burning Glass analysis of the optimal mix of career skills vividly illustrates the value of tailored, market-ready competencies when combined with a broader set of capabilities. The importance of the second part of this combination for progress through the labor market has been highlighted by

Harvard University economist David Deming. He groups a range of noncognitive skills, including teamwork, collaboration, and oral and written communications skills, under the heading "soft skills."[9] And he believes that the employment market is "way ahead of the ivory tower" in its emphasis on those abilities. While economists have devoted considerable attention to the role of pure cognitive skills in determining wages, employers consistently prize qualities such as the ability to work in a team, problem-solving skills, and written and verbal communication in new hires, he notes.

In part for these reasons, Deming has argued forcefully against "the impulse to make college curriculums ever more technical and career focused."[10] There's ample evidence that the popularity of college majors in the humanities has declined precipitously in recent decades—down 25 percent from 2012 to 2020, for example, to fewer than one in ten college graduates, even using an expansive definition of humanities that includes the popular "communications" major.[11] At the same time, the number of majors in fields like computer science has soared. But Deming makes the case that even the early earnings advantage of college graduates in STEM majors— science, technology, engineering, and mathematics—"fades steady" after their first postcollege jobs and that liberal arts majors gradually catch up by middle age.[12]

That's because the technical skills that garner a short-term salary premium become obsolescent and require refreshing over time. Meanwhile, Deming adds, the hard-to-quantify liberal arts soft skills like problem solving and adaptability have long-term career value "by design." At times of rapid technological change, he writes, range and flexibility are even more crucial: "A four-year college degree should prepare students for the next 40 years of working life, and for a future that none of us can imagine."[13]

His analysis is underscored by a survey of older and younger STEM workers conducted by an American Enterprise Institute team led by AEI senior fellow Brent Orrell. Those aged fifty to sixty-four were much more likely than their early-career counterparts under age thirty-five to call interpersonal skills and communications skills extremely important to do their jobs. The survey found a similar difference between higher-paid STEM workers making over $150,000 annually and those making less than $75,000 a year. "The lesson seems clear," Orrell writes in *Minding Our Workforce*, an edited volume on the importance of noncognitive skills. "A technical skill can help you get a job, but noncognitive skills are necessary to growing on the job."[14]

The same logic about the need to balance hard and soft skills can be applied not just to different kinds of college majors, but to the choice between a traditional college degree and the increasingly popular set of short-term, intensely practical, career-focused credentials. In an interview for the *Lessons Earned* podcast, Deming told me and cohost Aimée Eubanks Davis that the two kinds of skills complement one another. "If you have the ability to go get a four-year degree, you should do that. However, I think there's a rapidly burgeoning market of alternatives which can be additions to your education, not substitutions."[15]

Deming envisions a world "where more and more people are getting a four-year degree, and then also going to a coding boot camp, or to get a certificate in some specialized trade.

Because you're not really getting that specialized skill in a more general B.A. program." A world, one could say, that has a lot in common with what already exists at places like Colorado Mountain College and continues to take new forms at many other institutions.

Rising Demand for Nondegree Credentials: Maybe Degrees Are Overrated?

Long before the pandemic, public interest was strong and growing in short-term, affordable, career-focused, skills-based nondegree credentials. In a report released in the early months of the pandemic, the credit rating firm Moody's said that short-term credentials had made up 10 percent of total enrollment in 2018 and projected their market share would continue to grow quickly once Covid-19 had dissipated.[16]

During the same period, a series of nationally represented surveys conducted by Strada Education Network found a strong preference among Americans for nondegree and skills-based training during the pandemic. Meantime, as Paul Fain, a close industry watcher, reported for *Inside Higher Ed*, high-profile companies from Google and IBM to Salesforce and Microsoft announced their own bespoke short-term tech-focused credentials. Some tech employers began to say they were dropping degree requirements for certain jobs.[17]

The intense economic disruptions brought by the pandemic certainly accelerated the sense of urgency for advocates of short-term credentials. One prominent group of community college leaders and workforce analysts sent a letter to members of Congress in September 2021 seeking to make near-term, noncredit community college programs eligible for Title IV federal financial aid. "Midcareer adults whose jobs have been eliminated don't have time for a year or two of traditional academic education," wrote the group, whose signatories included Anne Kress, president of Northern Virginia Community College, Joe May, chancellor of Dallas College, Chauncy Lennon, vice president of Lumina Foundation, and Joseph Fuller, professor of management practice at Harvard Business School. "They need short, targeted bursts of training that enable them to reenter the labor force as quickly as possible."[18]

In an interview at his Harvard Business School (HBS) office, Fuller elaborated on his emphatic belief that today's system doesn't serve enough Americans well. The classic sequence—high school graduation, then on-time graduation from a four-year college, then obtaining a good job—simply isn't the reality for many. "The current system works very well for a minority of people, and pretty well for another tranche, and not really very well at all for everybody else, which is probably an absolute majority," he told me. The founder of the global consulting firm Monitor Group, now Monitor-Deloitte, Fuller now coleads HBS's Managing the Future of Work initiative.[19]

Young people require guidance early in life about what kinds of studies correlate with available jobs to ensure that they develop skills and a job history that puts their life trajectory in place, according to Fuller. Otherwise they risk getting stuck in a catch-22 in which lack of experience makes it harder to break into new fields. The short half-life of hard skills also means they will need refreshing over an individual's career.

Fuller is skeptical that traditional colleges can provide the kind of practical guidance and ongoing reskilling that many people require.

This complex mix of developments—uncertainty and anxiety about the market value of degrees, a strong public (and characteristically American) belief in practicality, the rising desire for inexpensive, short-term, job-oriented credentials, and the cataclysmic impact of the Covid-19 pandemic—combined to strengthen the push for BA alternatives. A contributing factor was the frequently heard argument made by Opportunity@Work, a new nonprofit founded by former McKinsey consultant and Obama administration official Byron Auguste. The group, and others sympathetic with its mission, maintains that excessive degree requirements for many jobs are thwarting opportunities for talented people, often disadvantaged minorities.

These individuals, described as STARS—skilled through alternative routes—may possess the actual skills needed to perform certain jobs successfully without holding the formal credentials listed as prerequisites. In June 2022, the group announced a national advertising campaign, in partnership with the Ad Council and corporate partners like Walmart and Google, to encourage employers to drop four-year degree requirements for job applicants, saying a "paper ceiling" is preventing half the US workforce from getting ahead even though they've developed skills in other ways, whether in certificate programs, through military service, in community college, or via on-the-job learning.[20] The credential barrier is a particular problem for African Americans and Latinos, who are substantially less likely than whites to hold bachelor's degrees.

Eventually, degree skeptics began to score some wins. In March 2022, the state of Maryland announced it was dropping bachelor's degree requirements for thousands of state jobs. And according to a study produced jointly by the Burning Glass Institute and several coauthors at Harvard Business School, this trend had already begun before the pandemic started and had made a serious dent in degree mandates. For "middle skill" jobs within the fifty-one million job postings in the analysis, 46 percent of ninety occupations studied saw a drop of more than 5 percent in bachelor's degree requirements from 2017 to 2019.[21] In another analysis published around the same time, RAND researcher Lindsay Daugherty summed up various findings about positive outcomes for certain nondegree credentials and uneven returns to certain degrees to argue that degree alternatives could be just as reliable a path to the middle class.[22]

Earnings Evidence and Revealed Preferences

But while there is ample evidence of public concern about the value of college, attention-getting figures showing a striking drop in enrollment, and a strong, much-discussed appetite for nondegree alternatives, none of these very real developments should be mistaken for a serious challenge to the well-deserved reputation college degrees hold as the gold standard of career credentials.

Extensive economic data, reviewed in the chapter that follows, documents the rising wage premium linked to college completion in the final decades of the twentieth century, an economic return that remains at an all-time-high when compared to average earnings of Americans with only a high school diploma.

In addition, a related and powerful measure of degree value relates to how employers actually use these credentials in the hiring process. Here, the conclusion is straightforward. Degrees matter for those making the decision to hire someone. To understand why, an instructive framework involves a different term favored by economists: "revealed preferences." It's a way of discussing the reality on the ground: How do individuals actually behave, regardless of what they say they value? When the Society for Human Resource Management (SHRM) conducted research into how employers feel about alternative credentials, it found that the rhetoric outpaces the reality.

In the summer of 2021, SHRM surveyed 500 executives, 1,200 supervisors, 1,129 human resource professionals, and 1,525 nonsupervisory workers about their views on increasingly popular nondegree credentials like certificates, badges, and apprenticeships. While all of the first three groups shared a positive view of alternative credentials, company leaders were much more likely to see those credentials as impressive and important in the hiring process than were hiring managers and HR professionals—who are directly involved in hiring new employees. For example, although 71 percent of executives said some alternative credentials are equivalent to a bachelor's degree, just 58 percent of supervisors and an even lower 36 percent of HR professionals agreed.[23]

The finding was underscored by an experiment SHRM conducted asking hiring managers to evaluate hypothetical job applicants with and without alternative credentials. Even when applicants who possessed alternative credentials had higher rankings on skills and would require less on-the-job training, those with traditional degrees had an advantage.

Strictly speaking, the SHRM study shows survey and experiment responses rather than real-world behavior. But it's highly suggestive of how people in a position to act directly are likely to make decisions. Whatever formal requirements might be included in an official job posting, in other words, candidates with degrees are likely to hold a significant edge when the time comes to make a hire. The much-heralded announcement about a reduction in how many state of Maryland jobs require bachelor's degree credentials (later followed by similar announcements in Utah, Pennsylvania, and New Jersey) may or may not translate into a significant increase in non–college graduates being hired.

Indeed, even shifts in formal job requirements are sometimes applauded so vigorously by advocates that their actual magnitude may be overstated. Consider the Burning Glass Institute study mentioned above, "The Emerging Degree Reset." It highlights considerable evidence that employers across industries, including in tech jobs at firms like IBM and Accenture, have loosened degree requirements for some high-skill jobs and even more middle-skill positions amid the pandemic. That includes occupations like customer service manager, paralegal, and billing clerk.[24]

The report argues that the changes started before Covid-19 and are likely to continue. Because the analysis looks at job postings and not actual hiring decisions, it's possible degree holders are still favored. But Sigelman told me he believes the lower requirements are "at least a decent proxy" for hiring behavior. "It's something they're reevaluating."[25] The data certainly fit nicely with the popular narrative that we are entering a new world of work, premised on rethinking what it takes to get hired, a story line welcomed by forward-looking thinkers as demonstrating the rise of new pathways into good jobs.

However, the Burning Glass report excluded more than half of fifty-one million job postings it studied to reach its conclusion. The study notes that it "eliminated from the analysis" occupations in which more than 90 percent of postings required a bachelor's or more. Why? Because such jobs "are highly unlikely to ever drop the degree requirement." Coauthor Sigelman, Burning Glass Institute president, told me the researchers wanted to account for fields like law, medicine, or chemical engineering in which continued degree requirements are uncontroversial. That exclusion left out 11.73 million job postings.[26] The analysis also excluded 24.7 million job postings in low-skill occupations in which fewer than 25 percent of postings required a bachelor's degree.

Of the remaining listings, when actual job postings rather than occupational categories were examined, a more modest 29 percent of middle-skill job postings and 17 percent of high-skill postings were in occupations with a "material degree reset," or a drop of more than 5 percent in bachelor's degree requirements from 2017 to 2019.[27] This suggests that the report's conclusion, while important, was somewhat more narrow than its framing suggested. Moreover, the Burning Glass Institute's chief economist posted an analysis at the end of 2022 indicating that, despite what employers may say in online job postings about removing degree requirements, they are actually hiring more, not fewer, college graduates.[28]

In addition, the report acknowledges a significant counter-vailing story line within its findings. Among new hires at leading firms such as Facebook, Apple, Microsoft, and Google, the share of positions in job postings requiring a bachelor's degree remains extremely high. Despite some decline since 2017, in 2021 nearly eight in ten information technology postings at Google and more than seven in ten at Apple specified a bachelor's or above. At Intel, the share of IT postings with a degree requirement actually rose from 87 to 96 percent. "There are a whole bunch of tech companies that continue to be pretty reliant on degrees," Sigelman said.

Yet big tech giants like Google and Microsoft have received enormous press fanfare in recent years for getting rid of degree requirements for new hires.[29] They had declared they would evaluate skills and promise, rather than require traditional credentials, when seeking new employees. In fact, it seems that reports of the demise of the bachelor's degree have gotten ahead of the facts on the ground. Contrary to the popular disruption story, companies like Google have not abandoned traditional credentials. Quite the opposite, says Sean Gallagher, founder of Northeastern University's Center for the Future of Higher Education and Talent Strategy: "they love college degrees."[30]

Maggie Johnson, Google's vice president of education and university programs, told me that although the company has created well-publicized Grow with Google online certificates for in-demand jobs in fields like digital marketing, IT support, and data analytics, those credentials aren't intended to prepare people to work at Google itself.[31] A former computer science professor at Stanford University, she says software engineers need deeper learning abilities than short-term programs typically provide. Although Google has made a small number of hires from top coding boot camps like Flatiron, General Assembly, and Bloomtech (formerly Lambda), those programs have modified their curriculum over the years to address the gap between four-year degrees and purely technical skills. They focus on verbal and written communication to prepare students for interviews, for example. Even so, Johnson says, "I still doubt that boot camp graduates can learn new languages and technologies as quickly as someone with a CS degree, but then not all companies have the requirements that Google has for its software engineers."[32]

There's definitely growing interest in skills-based hiring, particularly in today's tight labor market. But even that interest is somewhat deceptive. A lot of the growth and momentum in short-term credentials comes from people who already have degrees and are seeking additional targeted qualifications, Gallagher notes. In other words, the reality of the job market is much more complicated than the degree-is-dead narrative.

This disconnect matters for both practical and philosophical reasons. On the practical front, young people facing decisions about education need to know about the world as it is—not just the world hoped for by advocates of skills-based hiring. And despite some recent changes in occupational requirements, today's world still rewards degrees substantially. For all the chatter about college degrees being overrated, there remains a massive base of economic evidence for their value, not just for getting hired in the first place, but also for navigating what for many people are likely to be a series of job changes throughout a long career.

That brings us to the philosophy of degrees. It's not that they're perfect for everyone in all cases. As the next chapter will discuss in more detail, the positive data on economic returns to degrees—including an annual earning premium for college graduates of more than $30,000, or nearly 75 percent, compared to workers with only a high school diploma[33]—are about average salaries for degree-holders and don't represent any kind of across-the-board guarantee. What undergraduates study matters a lot for marketability, too. And far too many people start college and don't finish.

But those who actually acquire a college degree, including in liberal arts fields that take longer to pay off than STEM majors, frequently gain just the mix of broad skills and targeted skills required for career success. These skills include reading, writing, and analyzing in general ed classes followed by tailored instruction in fields like accounting, nursing, or computer science—or more academic study in the sciences or humanities before law school, medical school, or another graduate program.

But let's stipulate that a greater number of purposeful career-oriented options would be helpful and attractive to many students. What skeptics of the college access agenda often miss, when they declare knowingly that not everyone is cut out for college, is just how much vocational education *already* exists within the very large umbrella of our postsecondary system. Advocates of postsecondary education filled with purposeful, career-oriented options don't need to look far to find those in the US higher education system.

Consider our land-grant institutions, established in the second half of the nineteenth century with the explicit goal of providing more practical educational options for a fast-growing nation. Today, undergraduates at places like Iowa State University can major in fields such as animal science and dairy science, among many other agriculturally themed concentrations. Throughout the nation, it's completely unremarkable for undergrads to specialize in subjects like accounting, forensics, hotel management, and physical education. Plato around a seminar table this ain't. Yes, these four-year degrees typically require an academic grounding in a range of basic subjects under the heading "general education." Still, they are often overlooked by critics who imply that going to college will involve some kind of rarefied education that just won't serve many students.

The Case for a Both/And Approach to Degrees and Alternatives

So does the versatility and value of so many degrees mean that degree alternatives are a lost cause or irrelevant? Not at all. Many Americans are looking for faster and cheaper ways to boost their skills and improve their employment prospects. If they choose intelligently—such as in-demand health specialties, or data science, for instance—that strategy can work. To take just one example, Lumina Foundation's Chauncy Lennon points out that although half of employed adults with short-term certificates earn $30,000 or less per year, those who earn STEM certificates have higher average earnings than holders of associate degrees in education.[34]

What's more, a growing number of massive employers—Amazon and Walmart among them—will pay for short-term as well as traditional credentials, because they correctly view education as a useful employee-retention benefit in a tight labor market. When those short credentials can be stacked together into degrees with a track record of improving earnings over the long term, so much the better.

The challenge is for advocates of new pathways to the workforce not to depict degrees and degree alternatives as an either/or choice. That's a recipe for pushing people away from the credentials that are still, in the vast majority of cases, needed to land a job at Google or many other employers. Rather than sound a premature death knell for the degree, we should be calling for a both/and approach that acknowledges the complementary strengths of degrees and the best alternative credentials.

After all, it's quite true that in a both/and world many learners would benefit from robust, career-focused alternatives or supplements to college degrees. That's not because college is overrated, as critics misleadingly claim, but because a variety of opportunities can build human capital for more people in better ways. We need to think of traditional degrees and alternatives like short-term career training not as competing options but as different and *both* legitimate routes—for different people with diverse needs, or for the same person at different times in their life. That's why both/and is the new way, and the right way, to think about postsecondary education. Given the extensive evidence that so many fast-growing jobs require a combination of skills, from foundational abilities in writing and critical thinking to technical skills in areas like social media or IT networking, there's enormous potential to mix degrees with other kinds of credentials or skill-building opportunities. Liberal arts degrees, argues Sigelman of the Burning Glass Institute, have "twice as much value when combined with some specific technical skills."[35]

Giving students that empowering combination, whether through creative efforts at developing clusters of skills inside colleges or by encouraging supplemental skills acquisition, requires moving past what Sigelman calls the "lazy debate" between knowledge for its own sake and vocational skills.[36]

The resulting mixture of broad and targeted skills can be extremely useful for students' marketability and for their own satisfaction with the cost-effectiveness of their postsecondary education. A Strada Education Network–Gallup survey of more than eight thousand adults who had completed an associate degree or higher found that graduates who combined a college degree with a nondegree credential were more satisfied than their degree-only peers. They were more likely to agree or strongly agree that their credentials were "worth the cost," made them "an attractive job candidate," and "helped me achieve my goals." The differential was particularly high for those who had earned just an associate degree along with an alternative credential.[37]

For students eager to improve their near-term prospects, the right kinds of immediate educational offerings can serve as a stepping stone to a more optimal combination of market-ready and long-term skills. That's what Meghan Hughes has done as president of the Community College of Rhode Island. Her own experience combined formal academic training with a very practical perspective on what students need. She earned a PhD in Renaissance art history and started her career as a professor at Tufts University, followed by a stint as an executive at the workforce training organization Year Up. When she arrived at CCRI, says Hughes, "we were underserving our Rhode Island residents."[38]

Eager to generate opportunities for what she calls "a population that needed a job *right now*," she had a twin ambition: serving urgent needs while also forging valuable career pathways. "I'm never just going to create an opportunity for a job right now. I don't believe in it. I don't believe it's ethical." The question, she says, was this: "How do we give our young adults skills as quickly as possible to get them immediately into the workforce to start earning, while also showing them that they are college material—and while seeing them earn a significant percentage of what an associate degree is?" Now, under her leadership, CCRI offers certificates, created in partnership with employers, in fields like CNC manufacturing and finance. (CNC stands for computerized numerical control, a computerized manufacturing process in which software and code is used to preprogram the movement of production equipment.) The credits students earn give them a healthy fraction of what they'll need to get an associate degree.

Chapter 2 of this volume will review the strengths of college degrees, including the importance of completing. Chapter 3 highlights some of the best alternative credentials offered by community colleges, among others; describes training and work experience programs like Year Up; and shows how broad and targeted skills can be most usefully combined for career preparation, navigation, and lifelong success.

Needed: Social Capital

But although much work needs to be done to extend the college access movement to focus on higher completion rates, while boosting the respectability and usefulness of noncollege alternatives and supplements, these educational options remain necessary but not sufficient for many Americans. Large numbers of people, especially those from low-income and disadvantaged backgrounds, need to develop access to networks—and the ability to tap into those networks to connect their education and training to meaningful workforce opportunities.

These abilities to access and mobilize networks, often called social capital, are the subject of chapter 4. Social capital is the missing link for many who have followed all the rules about obtaining education to get ahead but still struggle to translate their skills into jobs with an upwardly mobile career path. In other words, while it's a cliche and not entirely accurate to declare that "it's not what you know, it's who you know," this old formula for career success is not entirely wrong either.

There is of course ample evidence that the development of more advanced skills in a changing economy is closely connected to the growing economic payoff of secondary and postsecondary education in the twentieth century and beyond, as documented by economists like Claudia Goldin and Lawrence Katz in their influential 2008 book *The Race between Education and Technology*.[39] But education and skills aren't enough for young people who lack the family and community connections that allow those from more privileged backgrounds to learn about a range of professional pathways, try them out and demonstrate their abilities through summer jobs and internships, and get hired for jobs with real growth potential. Indeed, the value of getting career-oriented work experience while studying, sometimes called experiential learning, is widely recognized; a majority of students now complete an internship before graduation. The feedback and networks that come with internships are invaluable—yet it often takes a network to identify a promising internship opportunity.

Unfortunately, much of our attention has been focused in less vital directions. For example, college skeptics continue to fret that young people in high school are being funneled into traditional academic institutions when they would be better off pursuing practical, career-oriented alternatives such as apprenticeships. Meantime, nonprofits and schools spend more than $600 million annually to teach financial literacy.[40] Yet as pointed out by Edward DeJesus, founder of an organization called Social Capital Builders, much less energy has been devoted to helping students build the networks that would help them turn all kinds of academic and practical skills into employment opportunities.

The result is that from high school to college to the crucial years after college, huge numbers of students build academic and career skills without receiving the kind of support they need to create, nurture, and expand a very different but extremely important set of skills and networks. In a July 2020 Gallup survey of college alumni who had graduated in the past decade, the highest percentage—nearly half—picked networking as the skill in which they wish they had received more training during their undergraduate years.[41] Many organizations described in chapter 4 are tackling the problem using diverse tactics.

Those might include helping first-generation undergraduates feel that they really belong in college, as the nonprofit Beyond 12 does, and showing them how networks of peers and professors can help them thrive on campus. It could also entail the kind of programming the organization Braven offers to show low-income college students how to present their strengths in job applications and how to seek meetings with employment contacts who are often all too happy to discuss their own career trajectories and offer advice when asked.

Or it could be the postcollege coaching, tailored sector-specific skill preparation, and peer support provided by COOP Careers to students who may never have received career assistance in college as basic as help strengthening their LinkedIn profiles. Founder Kalani Leifer still remembers "marinating" in social capital as a Stanford undergraduate who literally grew up on the Palo Alto campus as the son of a mechanical engineering professor.[42] He and others just want to equip students with fewer inherited network advantages with some of the same access to professional connections their more affluent peers have acquired largely by happenstance.

These reforms aren't always straightforward, of course. Many college students are hungry for professors to help them make professional connections and learn about internships and job opportunities. But despite some promising new initiatives, not all professors see explicit career preparation as part of *their* jobs. For their part, not all students are ready to embrace the notion that developing connections should be part of what they seek in college or through alternative credentials.

Ann Kirschner, professor of practice at Arizona State University and former dean of the City University of New York's Macaulay Honors College, says many of the first-generation students she has known view networking as something akin to cheating—a shortcut that isn't entirely reputable compared to traditional measures of academic accomplishment.

My final chapter sums up the eight career arts for people making choices about education and careers, and for all those who want to offer these individuals their informed support.

The initial three career arts are recommended practices that underscore, first, the value of college: "Go to College (Yes, It's a Good Idea)"; second, the need to find the right institution and program: "Find the Best *Kind* of College and Program"; and third, the importance of graduating: "Complete College."

The fourth career art is aimed at people not on the traditional college track: "If Pursuing Nondegree Options, Purposefully Build Education, Skills, and Networks." The fifth career art, "Seek a Both/And Combination of Broad and Targeted Skills," stresses the need to challenge head-on the philosopher/welder stereotype that creates an unhelpful and false dichotomy when people need to make crucial choices about all kinds of education and training possibilities. Reflecting the concrete examples and stories scattered throughout the book, it calls on educators, parents, and students to embrace broad education and targeted career preparation as a both/and proposition rather than the either/or trade-off that too often dominates public debate.

The sixth career art is intensely practical, advising working adults: "Take Advantage of Employer-Funded Education Benefits." The seventh career art calls for adding career networking, broadly defined, to the mix—"Find Effective Ways to

Build Social Capital"—to maximize the power of following all the other advice about building credentials and skills. Finally, the eighth career art stresses the importance of following the best available evidence about what degrees, skills, and networks usually lead to success, rather than being sidetracked by wishful thinking: "Prepare for the World as It Is, Not as You Wish It Were."

In the end, we need to reject the straw man claims that a "college for all" movement is constricting a healthier range of educational choices. It would be more accurate to say that in recent decades American schools have placed a higher premium on the goal of college *readiness* for many more students. (Plenty of practical coursework options are still available. According to the National Center for Education Statistics, in the 2016–17 school year 98 percent of public school districts around the country offered career and technical education, or CTE, to high school students.[43] And some CTE coursework can be combined with postsecondary classes.)

Similarly, we should set aside the blue collar romance built into calls for expanded vocational training for jobs like plumbing and truck driving. Nor, to be sure, should we expect that a conventional academic route to a traditional college degree will be the right fit for everyone. Rather than persist in a public dialogue that causes anxiety and uncertainty among ordinary Americans, we should clearly identify the mixture of broad education, targeted skills, and active professional networks that can help individuals and the nation get ahead. That is the rich, varied combination of academic preparation and work readiness that savvy students can and should embrace in the real world.

Chapter 2

Degree Value

Susan Dynarski was considered a troublemaker in high school. The daughter of working-class parents in Somerville, Massachusetts—her father was a mechanic for the US Postal Service, her mother a phlebotomist for a Veterans Administration hospital—she didn't seem to have an elite education in her future. She was on the non–honors track at Matignon High School, a Catholic school in Cambridge. And although she worked as a waitress at Brigham's Ice Cream, she had never once set foot in Harvard Yard just across the street.

But her trajectory changed after the results of her SAT college-entrance exams came in. The nuns who ran her school "hadn't seen scores like mine," she says.[1] Before long she was encouraged to set her academic sights high and ultimately enrolled as an undergraduate at Harvard. Generous financial aid and a work-study job made the out-of-pocket costs less than at the University of Massachusetts–Boston, where her older sisters had gone to college.

Her path wasn't entirely smooth. She landed on academic probation when, for want of good advising, the aspiring engineer took four STEM classes, including chemistry, calculus, and computer programming, in the same semester. Having previously never met affluent people, she also felt considerable culture shock in her privileged surroundings. "Washing dishes for my classmates was a formative experience," she says drily of her dining hall job. More comfortable with campus clerical and technical workers than with many of her fellow students, she became a union organizer. Ultimately, she earned a PhD in economics at the Massachusetts Institute of Technology, taught at the Kennedy School of Government and the University of Michigan, became a regular *New York Times* contributor, and is now back at Harvard as a tenured professor and a leading national authority on expanding college access and affordability.

Along the way, she became an advocate for universal ACT and SAT testing for high school students as a tool for narrowing the income gap in who attends selective colleges. Research in Michigan and other states, in an echo of her own experience, found that standardized tests identified many academically promising students. "A lot of high-scoring poor kids popped up," she told me over dinner at a Massachusetts Avenue restaurant.[2] Many who wouldn't have taken the tests without a universal requirement ultimately enrolled and graduated from college.[3] Dynarski also played a prominent role as an advocate of simplifying the Free Application for Federal Student Aid, or FAFSA. "Many smart students forgo college in the mistaken belief that they cannot afford it," she wrote in a 2015 *New York Times* column.[4] "The financial aid system, which is intended to increase opportunities for low-income students, is largely to blame."

Her work is premised on the value of attending and graduating from college. Dynarski doesn't have much patience for those who argue that too many people go to college and that the evidence for its benefits has been exaggerated. As an economist, she sees the evidence as open and shut in most cases. "My catchphrase is 'There's never been a worse time to *not* be a college graduate,'" she says. That's partly because a large portion of the increase in the economic returns to college since the 1970s has come not because of real earnings for college graduates rising but instead because the real earnings of high school graduates have plummeted. "You're still better off going to college." She is unimpressed by surveys showing the growing popularity of nondegree credentials. If employers cared less about degrees and stopped requiring them, she reasons, that would show up in the economic data as a lower average salary payoff for bachelor's degrees. So far, it has not.

The consensus that postsecondary education is essential to promote economic opportunities and upward mobility was authoritatively demonstrated by economists Goldin and Katz when they argued that the growth in demand for better-educated workers that took place during the twentieth century was driven by skill-based technological change.[5] The high school movement in the first part of the century increased the relative supply of more-educated workers and actually reduced the high school wage premium. By the mid-twentieth century, education levels continued to grow quickly and skills kept pace with demand.

However, from 1980 to 2005 the relative supply of educated Americans slowed, and the college wage premium skyrocketed. As a result, Goldin and Katz write, "the marginal individual today who does not graduate high school, who does not continue to college, and who does not complete college, is leaving large amounts of money lying on the street." The growth rate of the college wage premium has flattened in the past fifteen years, but it remains very high even as a high school diploma alone becomes less and less valuable.[6] Recent data from the Federal Reserve Bank of New York found a record $22,000 annual earnings gap between recent college graduates and those with less education. Median income for bachelor's degree holders aged twenty-two to twenty-seven reached $52,000 annually in 2021, compared to $30,000 for high school graduates in the same age range.[7] Another relevant data point: job losses during the Covid-19 pandemic were much steeper for workers with a high school diploma or less, and employment recovery was much slower.

Some critics of expanding college attendance argue that certain lower-achieving students don't belong in college. However, researchers have found that college provides significant economic benefits even to relatively low performing students. Seth D. Zimmerman studied students who fell just above and just below the academic requirements for admission to Florida International University. Those who attended college had better long-term economic outcomes than those who didn't, particularly men and people from low-income households.[8] Another study published in the *Journal of Labor Economics* used data from thirteen public universities in Ohio that dismiss students based on a grade point average cutoff. Low-performing students just above the cutoff who persisted recouped their educational investment and saw substantial earnings gains eight years after the dismissal of their similar classmates who were just below the cutoff.[9]

That said, positive average economic returns to higher education are certainly not identical across individuals and institutions. As analysts like economist Anthony Carnevale of Georgetown University's Center on Education and the Workforce have detailed, academic programs and majors in fields with high market demand, including STEM subjects such as engineering or computer science, typically lead to higher earnings.[10]

For example, a recent analysis by Third Way found that 100 percent of nursing and engineering graduates were able to recoup their educational investment within five years, compared to 45 percent of religious studies students and 44 percent of anthropology graduates. Overall, the study found, close to two-thirds of all programs allowed students to recoup their educational costs within a decade of graduation, but 16 percent left graduates with no return on investment at all.[11]

Similarly, the specific subject studied matters so much for near-term employability that it can be a countervailing factor to the general observation that more years of education correlate with greater return on investment: adults with short-term STEM certificates earn more, on average, than those with associate degrees in education. Yet over time less career-focused subjects tend to pay off, as Harvard economist David Deming points out. The STEM advantages "fades steadily" after graduates' first jobs, he writes, "and by age 40 the earnings of people who majored in fields like social science or history have caught up."[12]

Community colleges are another particularly useful set of institutions from which to observe how the combination of market demand and subject studied can lead to significantly varying outcomes. As Carnevale noted in an interview,[13] certified nursing assistant credentials are "a standard community college product" for which demand is very high, but wages are "lousy."

Adding to concerns about the low market value of certain subjects commonly studied at community colleges is the demographic of the students who disproportionately enroll in those fields, says Josh Wyner, founder and executive director of the College Excellence Program at the Aspen Institute, which works closely with community college presidents and other higher education leaders. "Where are the Black and Latino students, the women? They're in low-wage CTE [career and technical education] programs," he told me. "If you look at who is in what programs, you invariably find that the highest-value programs, the programs that lead to the greatest success in the workforce after you leave or after you transfer, are overwhelmingly populated by white, wealthier students."[14]

Those higher-value programs do provide distinctly more lucrative payoffs. Carnevale's Center on Education and the Workforce found in a 2020 report, "The Overlooked Value of Certificates and Associate's Degrees," that workers who hold associate degrees in engineering have median earnings between $50,000 and $60,000, about twice as high as workers with associate degrees in education and the arts.[15] Differential returns by field of study also explain why a community college associate degree in certain majors can yield higher earnings than some bachelor's degrees. Associate degree holders who studied engineering, for example, command median earnings that significantly outpace the $30,000 to $40,000 annual income of those with bachelor's degrees in education.[16]

But of course that's not the end of the story. For all the evidence that degrees generally provide significant benefits, higher education has frequently failed to deliver on the outcomes students were anticipating. In 1975, 49 percent of American high school graduates went on to some form of postsecondary education immediately after finishing school. Four decades later, that figure had soared to a record 70 percent. Unfortunately, this impressive increase in access to college hasn't been accompanied by correspondingly higher success in bringing students across the finish line. Comparing the high school class of 1972 to the class of 1992, significantly higher college attendance rates were accompanied by a 4.6 percentage point decline in completion rates.[17]

Although graduation rates began moving up again from 1990 to 2010,[18] they remain disappointing: Only 62 percent of first-time, full-time undergraduates at four-year institutions complete a degree at that institution within six years. Six-year graduation rates are significantly worse for Hispanic students (57 percent) and Black students (42 percent), who will make up a growing percentage of the US population and workforce in the twenty-first century. For students from low-income families who receive federal Pell grants, the graduation gap is similarly stark: more than 10 percentage points lower at public institutions and close to 15 percentage points lower at private colleges.[19] Completion rates for part-time students and those in two-year community colleges are even worse. Eighty percent of the 1.7 million students who start community college each year say they plan to earn at least a bachelor's degree. But just one-third of those who started in fall 2007 transferred to a four-year college, and only 14 percent got a bachelor's degree within six years.[20] This disconnect between aspirations and actual completion figures thwarts the potential earnings prospects of noncompleters, particularly in liberal arts, where a successful transfer followed by completion of a bachelor's degree is crucial to maximizing the future economic value of this pathway.[21]

Such high rates of noncompletion explain why some thirty-nine million working-age adults report their highest level of education as "some college, no degree."[22] Those who took out loans for their education thus face the unenviable combination of student debt without a degree to help position them to repay what they owe.

Even among college graduates, critics argue that significant numbers are underemployed, taking jobs that don't require degrees, or shouldn't. More broadly, they complain that there is too often a lack of clear connections between the skills acquired in a range of undergraduate programs and those needed by employers, particularly in high-growth fields such as health care and information technology.

For too long, the Aspen Institute's Wyner says, colleges and universities had a mind-set focused solely on access, or perhaps access plus completion—what he refers to as the first two phases of the student-success movement, College 1.0 and 2.0, respectively. It's time for them to embrace what he terms College 3.0, where three vital measures go together: access plus completion *plus success.*

Now, anxiety about the value of higher education driven by concerns about insufficient college-career links has been compounded by the disruption of the Covid-19 epidemic and the broad reassessment of employment commonly called the Great Resignation. Add demographic shifts reducing the number of traditional-age students, together with recent economic growth providing more near-term job opportunities that may provide an appealing alternative to college, and current enrollment declines are enormous.

The numbers are stark. The college and university enrollment decline of 1.4 million students since the pandemic has added to the struggles facing many institutions. In 2021 alone, according to estimates from the National Student Clearinghouse, full-time enrollment at community colleges has dropped 9.8 percent[23] on top of a 27 percent enrollment decline in the decade before 2019.[24] Undergraduate enrollment among twenty-five- to twenty-nine-year-olds has gone down by 8.3 percent.[25]

Yet it would be counterproductive for individuals, and bad for the country, if Americans avoided higher education for the wrong reasons and were left as a result without the human capital they need to flourish. It may not be possible to alter certain long-standing economic trends, like the countercyclical pattern of college enrollment falling when employment opportunities become stronger. But it should be possible to make the case for a range of postsecondary options beyond high school that are increasingly helpful for developing the skills needed in a changing economy. The reality of the postsecondary education experience is very different from what many critics, and even some supporters, believe.

For one thing, the wide range of institutions under the huge umbrella of our higher education system—from community colleges and state land-grant universities to elite private research institutions—already includes many career-building opportunities, including development of technical and vocational skills. Take Richard Rosendale, a prominent chef who represented the United States in the Bocuse d'Or, a high-powered global culinary competition. He was a middling student in high school and went on to earn an associate degree from the culinary program at Westmoreland County Community College in Youngwood, Pennsylvania. There, many students work as apprentices in restaurants and hotels while also taking degree requirements that include industry-specific skills like baking and beverage management as well as college writing, computing, and social science or math.[26]

What's more, although it's true that employers sometimes want new hires to have immediate job-ready skills, many also seek those with key general skills, including judgment, adaptability, teamwork, and the ability to communicate clearly. Such general skills are vital for long-term career advancement, and degree holders often develop them, which is one reason employers reward college graduates with significantly higher average wages. Labor market analysts note that recent in-demand skills include project management, strategic planning, marketing, writing, and sales—all suggesting that a specific major matters less than broad, transferable abilities. Little wonder that the managing director of global investment firm BlackRock told a group of college presidents that his best employees are those who are able to operate outside of silos and speak to many different people. "That sounds roughly like a liberal arts education," he said.[27]

Despite all the employers who see value in liberal arts degrees, and notwithstanding the evidence for their long-term economic returns cited by Deming and others, the general public's view of these subjects is often one of concern or misunderstanding. The liberal arts have their origins in classical Greek and Roman civilization as a collective term for the skills a free person needs to participate in public life. At medieval European universities, the seven liberal arts were defined as grammar, rhetoric, and logic (the trivium) along with geometry, arithmetic, music, and astronomy (the quadrivium).[28] Today, liberal arts are often thought of as the general education component of a college education as distinct from vocational fields. They include literature, philosophy, history, and other humanities subjects, but also physical and biological sciences, mathematics, and social sciences such as political science and sociology.

Unfortunately, for many Americans the contemporary perception of the term includes the notion of liberal as left leaning and arts as lacking any practical career value—adding up to what Brandon Busteed, then a Gallup executive, once called "a branding disaster." He cited a survey in which US parents with children in middle and high school rated "no college at all" as better than a liberal arts degree in providing a path to a good job. In Gallup marketing tests, he added, "phrases such as '21st century skills' test far better than 'liberal arts'—despite their very similar descriptions."[29]

Beyond the public's dim view of the liberal arts, its reaction to a seemingly more straightforward concept—whether a college degree is worth the money it costs individuals—is also distinctly mixed. In September 2021, the American Association of Colleges and Universities (AAC&U) and the Bipartisan Policy Center released a joint analysis of a survey of 2,220 American adults and compared their views with another recent poll focused on employers. Fully 87 percent of employers said a degree is "definitely" or "probably" worth the investment. Among the general public, the overall figure is considerably lower—a small majority of 60 percent agree the investment is worthwhile. Differences by income, education, and political party were particularly striking. Close to three-quarters of respondents who possess a bachelor's degree said the credential is worth the time and money invested, very similar to the 74 percent of those with an annual income above $100,000 who held this view. Just 51 percent of those without a college degree and 52 percent of those with an annual income below $50,000 believe college is worth the investment. A similar split occurs along partisan lines, with seven in ten Democrats seeing bachelor's degrees as financially worthwhile compared to just over 50 percent of Republicans and independents.[30]

Changing public opinion isn't easy, but it is badly needed in the case of college value given the high stakes involved. Naysayers notwithstanding, expanding college access and increasing completion rates should be a national priority. The compelling base of research showing the positive economic returns to college in part reflects the way college degrees often help develop a very useful mix of broad and targeted skills required for career success. It cannot be stated often enough that despite rising tuition and student debt loads, the lifetime earnings of bachelor's degree holders are 75 percent higher than they were thirty years ago.[31] Observers like Laura d'Andrea Tyson, former director of the National Economic Council and a professor at the Haas School of Business at the University of California, Berkeley, note that the financial returns to a college education significantly exceed the payoff to investments such as stocks, bonds, housing, and gold.[32]

Reminding Americans of this evidence to guide their decisions does not mean universities are without significant weaknesses. Many are much less effective than they should be at retaining and graduating students, and providing undergraduates with the education and skills they need to succeed in life. But the answer is not to embrace skepticism about the value of degrees, misleading the public. There is more reason than ever for Americans to seek out postsecondary opportunities, for policy makers to foster college access, and for colleges and universities themselves to include and succeed with more students.

History

For as long as prominent thinkers have pondered the purpose of education, they have been preoccupied by the practical versus the larger ends of knowledge. As Earl Cheit writes in *The Useful Arts and the Liberal Tradition*, his 1975 book on professional schools, "the tension between what is 'liberal' and what is 'useful' is one of the oldest and most persistent problems in education." He quotes Aristotle's *Politics*, in which the philosopher asked, "Should the useful in life, or should virtue, or should the higher knowledge be the aim of our training?"[33] Aristotle's conclusion was inconclusive: "All three opinions have been entertained . . . [yet] no one knows on what principle we should proceed."

With the advent of Western universities in cities such as Bologna, Paris, and Oxford in the Middle Ages, classical notions of the liberal arts firmly shaped the pursuit of knowledge. By the time the first American university, Harvard, was founded in 1636 to educate ministers during the Puritan era, its mission reflected the English university model, with a 1650 charter calling for "the advancement of all good literature, artes, and Sciences." Requirements included Latin, Greek, and Hebrew, with other disciplines including rhetoric and logic, ethics and politics, arithmetic and geometry, and eventually astronomy, physics, and metaphysics.[34]

Yet as early as the first part of the nineteenth century, Cheit reports, the *Edinburgh Review* found fault with Oxford's classical education "for its remoteness from practical life."[35] Over time, a multiplicity of educational practices and aims began to characterize universities. In the United States, following the Civil War, the land-grant university movement formally launched with the Morrill Act of 1862 firmly integrated Cheit's "useful arts" into the nation's higher education tradition. The rise and expansion of institutions devoted to agricultural, technical, and scientific education were enormously influential. "During the ten years after 1863," writes Laurence R. Veysey in his authoritative history *The Emergence of the American University*, "almost every visible change in the pattern of American higher education lay in the direction of concessions to the utilitarian type of demand for reform."[36]

This yearning for practicality, accompanied by the influence of the German research university model with the open-
ing of universities like Johns Hopkins University, helped lead
to both highly specialized undergraduate degrees and faculty
emphasis on research within disciplines and departments.[37]
These trends coexisted uneasily within the intellectual heri-
tage of universities, leading to concerns, as Christopher Jencks
and David Riesman wrote in *The Academic Revolution*, "that
specialization has gotten out of hand, that knowledge was becoming too fragmented, that research was being overemphasized, and that the transcendent truths and eternal verities
were being lost in the process."[38] An effort to restore balance
emerged in the 1920s in the form of the general education
movement, which aimed to provide students who had not yet
decided on a specific profession with a range of courses, not
necessarily a common curriculum but one selected from distribution requirements across several fields of study.

As the curriculum continued to be debated and recali-
brated, US higher education grew by leaps and bounds. The
GI Bill opened the doors to college for millions of World War
II veterans (though with much poorer outcomes for Black veterans from the South).[39] By the early 1970s, those numbers
had been expanded by a "tidal wave" of community college
students, in the words of Roger Geiger, a leading historian of
higher education. During that roughly three-decade period,
he writes, the proportion of young Americans attending college tripled from 15 to 45 percent, with the 1960s registering
the highest percentage growth of any decade.[40]

With college-going vastly more common than it was one
hundred years ago, both the rationale for general education
and its weaknesses have continued to be the subject of consid-

erable discussion. Still some version of this system remains common for today's US undergraduates. Students are commonly required to take some mixture of introductory courses in writing, natural science, quantitative reading, humanities, and social science before picking a major that might range from the intensely practical—accounting, nursing, or computer science, for example—to something more purely academic, such as physics or philosophy.

Thus the evolution of US universities, contrary to the ivory tower stereotype, may position graduates from the traditional liberal arts or from explicitly preprofessional programs for a wide range of next steps. Some may enter the workforce immediately, whether in an entry-level position open to graduates with broad skills or a more specialized position for which a degree in data science, hotel management, finance, or forensics might be a common prerequisite. Others may go on to specialized graduate study in law, medicine, business, engineering, or any number of fields leading to careers in scientific research or academia. In all these cases, the benefits of a bachelor's degree, with its characteristic mix of general and targeted education, are widely recognized as a proven building block for many careers.

Return on Investment, How Major Choice Impacts Opportunity for Disadvantaged Students, and Responding to the Skeptics

For those who have accepted the broad evidence demonstrating the value of college degrees, the discussion is far from over. Many related questions remain, to which the answers aren't simple. The debate is all the more urgent for those who remain skeptical about whether the apparent benefits of college are in fact an artifact of factors unrelated to what students learn.

Let's begin with the often-discussed notion of return on investment for a college education. Rising costs and student debt have made this an especially pressing matter for many current students, potential students, and policy makers. We know there is wide variation in which fields of study lead to the strongest economic returns for graduates. When choice of major is held constant, which specific institutions yield the strongest return on investment? The subheading of an article in the *Chronicle of Higher Education* gives a sense of the complications of the topic: "The Imperfect Science and Contested Methods of Measuring the Return on Investment of College."[41]

When looking at return on investment (ROI) across colleges, numerous studies using a range of methodologies come to varying conclusions. In October 2021, the center-left think tank Third Way published "Paying the Right Price for Your College Program,"[42] which used a metric developed by the organization, the "Price-to-Earnings Premium," to compare out-of-pocket costs at a given college to the expected additional income a typical graduate of a specific program is likely to earn. The idea is to evaluate how long it will take a student to recover what they have spent on their education. In one of several illustrative case studies, the report shows that a psychology major at the University of Texas at Dallas, a large public university, would see significantly higher return on investment than a psychology graduate at Southern Methodist University, a small private college.

The math works out as follows: If a psychology student at UT Dallas graduates in four years, her out-of-pocket costs will come to $57,300. On average, her earnings would be $9,300 more each year than a Texas high school graduate with no college experience. Using those figures, Third Way estimates it would take her 6.2 years to recoup her costs. By contrast, the typical psychology student at SMU would pay nearly three times as much—$146,300—for a four-year degree and would see average earnings just $3,500 per year more than a Texas high school graduate who didn't attend college. It would take more than forty-one years for that student to recover her costs, or almost seven times longer than her UT Dallas counterpart. "Two well-known colleges in Dallas, two identical degrees, two extremely different outcomes," the report concludes.

Using this methodology, Third Way's study reached the striking conclusion that fully 10 percent of bachelor's degree programs and 21 percent of associate degree programs offer no return on investment. Inevitably, however, the specific time frame used to analyze degree payoff influences the results. Third Way used data from the federal government's College Scorecard, which Third Way senior fellow in higher education Michael Itzkowitz had been instrumental in developing when he worked for the US Department of Education. With only two years of program-level earnings data available when the study was conducted, the time frame necessarily reflected only short-term results. As noted in the *Chronicle*, engineering and health majors would yield high returns in the near term, whereas a graduate in fields like biology, English, or sociology from highly selective Carleton College would appear to receive no economic ROI. "For most of those students at Carleton," author Scott Carlson wrote, "the picture is probably very different 10 years out."[43]

Another study, released a few months later by Georgetown University's Center on Education and the Workforce, seemed to show even more dire results for many colleges using a longer time line—10 years after enrollment. On average, six in ten college students across all institutions earn more than a high school graduate after ten years, the February 2022 study found. At 30 percent of colleges, or 1,233 institutions, more than half of students earn *less* than a high school graduate ten years after enrolling.[44] The center released an online tool that featured ROI rankings of forty-five hundred colleges and universities using new College Scorecard data.

A major factor in the center's conclusion, however—easily missed in the headlines about the report—is that its analysis includes all students who enrolled and not just those who graduated. Given high noncompletion rates at many institutions, the low ROI is much more a reflection of the danger of not graduating than a commentary on the poor economic return of such a high proportion of degrees earned. Center director Anthony Carnevale captured this distinction in his statement accompanying the report's release:

> College typically pays off, but the return on investment varies by credential, program of study, and institution. It's important to inform people about the risk of taking out loans but not graduating, which could leave them without the increased earnings that would help them repay those loans.[45]

Still another approach to comparing students' economic outcomes after graduating from different institutions entails focusing on the characteristics of the undergraduates themselves. This kind of analysis has particular relevance to the long-standing question of whether elite institutions produce strong labor market outcomes because of what they achieve educationally or simply because of which students they enroll. A classic study examining economic returns by institution type, by Stacy Berg Dale and the late Princeton University economist Alan Krueger, published in the *Quarterly Journal of Economics* in 2002,[46] tackled this problem by comparing comparably qualified students who applied to and were accepted by similarly highly selective colleges. They found that students at elite colleges had "about the same" earnings as those who were admitted to comparable colleges but opted to attend less selective schools. The only exception was among students from low-income families, who earned more if they attended selective colleges. That may be, as Dale and Krueger argued in a later paper, because those disadvantaged students were able to access otherwise unavailable networks at highly selective institutions.[47] Overall, when it comes to future earnings, the characteristics that accrue to incoming students seem to trump institutional differences.

For many students, this research suggests, choice of institution—highly selective private college versus a state's flagship public university, for example—may make little difference to future earnings. By contrast, choice of subject studied in college, no matter at which institution, can be decisive when it comes to return on investment, particularly in the near term. That core observation, together with the steps that can be taken to link college studies more purposefully to career opportunity, has significant implications for improving upward mobility through higher education for disadvantaged students.

On the one hand, there's clearly considerable work to be done to improve lagging retention and graduation rates for low-income and minority students. At the same time, those improved educational results are not by themselves sufficient to significantly narrow income inequality through better career outcomes. Universities should do much more to focus not simply on campus representation of first-generation and low-income students and students of color, but on ensuring that those students are positioned for later workforce success, argue Matt Sigelman, president of the Burning Glass Institute, and Christopher B. Howard, former president of Robert Morris University and now an executive vice president of Arizona State University.

In a January 2022 white paper, "Dynamos for Diversity," the two found that Black and Hispanic students are "disproportionately concentrated in majors with lower earnings." That in turn means they are more likely than their white and Asian peers after graduation to be underemployed, defined as someone with a bachelor's degree holding a job that typically doesn't require one.[48] Sigelman and Howard also note that Black and Latino undergraduates are less likely than others to get hands-on work experience via internships. Those vital career-building experiences are associated with a 9 percent greater likelihood of holding a job after graduation that requires a bachelor's degree. And the advantages of internships are even greater for underrepresented minorities in certain STEM majors: Black students in computer science and IT majors who secure internships are almost 30 percent more likely to hold jobs after graduation that require a bachelor's degree, while Latino students are 26 percent more likely.[49]

It's quite true that financial returns are far from the only meaningful outcome of attending and graduating from college. Valuable professions such as teaching and social work are often cited as worthwhile career paths for individuals and for society that don't entail maximizing a graduate's annual salary. Yet as Sigelman and Howard note, it would be "naive to downplay [the] importance" of economic prosperity as a hoped-for outcome of college, all the more so for racial and ethnic groups that consistently lag behind others.[50] They call on institutions to make equity a reality for disadvantaged undergraduates over the long term by encouraging those students to consider majors with stronger return on investment, and also by helping them find internships that will help boost their career prospects.

This move would not be without controversy, they warn, but it is nevertheless crucial. "Any suggestion that colleges encourage students to major in academic disciplines with better career outcomes is likely to be met with opposition on campuses from those departments that see these choices as a zero-sum game," they write. "But it's not. It's about college leaders promoting career fields that historically have lacked diversity in part because universities have left the onus on student success to the students themselves. Now, helping students is both a moral and financial imperative for institutions."[51]

Signaling

The long-term trend of enormously positive average payoffs to college degrees is unmistakable. There have certainly been periods of retrenchment or stalling. Economist Richard Freeman's influential 1976 volume *The Overeducated American* analyzed the declining college wage premium of the 1970s,[52] which was thought to have dire implications for colleges and universities—until the trend reversed dramatically in the 1980s. The run-up in wages for college-educated workers since then has been considerable, although male graduates' earnings have remained relatively flat since 2002 and overall wages since then have been driven by continued earnings growth for women with degrees.[53] Moreover, among younger Americans ages twenty-five to thirty-four, far more women than men now hold bachelor's degrees—46 percent compared to 36 percent.[54] In addition, as Dynarski told me, the overwhelming financial advantages to holding a college degree has been attributable in recent years not to a continued rise in real earnings for college graduates but to the decline in earnings for those who hold only a high school diploma or less.[55]

Nevertheless, as Adam Looney, a former Treasury Department official now at the University of Utah and the Brookings Institution, observes, whether judged by the annual earnings of well-educated Americans with bachelor's, master's, doctoral or professional degrees, or the earnings gap between individuals with just a high school diploma and those with a bachelor's degree, "the economic benefit to a college degree has, in fact, never been larger."[56]

But why? Two main schools of thought offer distinct explanations for the earnings premium associated with college in recent decades. They are not mutually exclusive and not always easy to disentangle. The human capital theory holds that the substantive knowledge and skills acquired through education translate into higher productivity and thus higher wages. The signaling theory suggests that a degree may be a proxy for other characteristics, unrelated to the actual education obtained in college but useful for employers who may be looking for shorthand measures of talent. In both cases, individuals with talent and potential obtain additional education, which contributes to the difficulty of separating the impact of substance and signal.

Signaling has been a particularly popular theory among iconoclasts like Bryan Caplan, author of *The Case against Education*,[57] who chalks up the economic returns to education to the ability degrees offer to signal to employers that those who have earned them possess characteristics such as intelligence, conscientiousness, and an ability to fit in with others. And it's widely accepted among economists that signaling certainly plays a role in explaining the college wage premium—perhaps as much as 20 percent or even one-third—because of the imperfect information available in the short run to firms hiring new employees.

But the notion that signaling is the primary explanatory factor behind the earning power of college degree holders is dismissed by experts like Katz. In an interview, he reeled off examples of instances in which expanded access to education, as well as compulsory schooling laws, have rapidly led to improved productivity and economic advancement. "When we built a high school in Iowa in the 1920s, and then saw a 20 percent improvement in agricultural productivity, that is not because we were signaling to the soil that we have high school education. We actually learned something about the science, and how to take up new sorts of fertilizers."[58] Something similar happened in India, when broadened school attendance during the twentieth century helped lead to the Green Revolution and an improved food supply. By the same token, when the English school-leaving age was extended from fourteen to fifteen after World War II, wages rose by about 14 percent,[59] suggesting that employers saw greater market value in what students had learned.

A much more recent example came in 2006 when the most selective university in Colombia, Universidad de Los Andes, reduced the number of credits required to earn degrees in economics and business. The university dropped twelve required courses in economics and six mandatory courses in business. Total instruction time was reduced from four and a half years to four. During the same period, however, admission standards, which rely on students' scores on a standardized national high school exit exam, remained the same. So did the size of the entering class. Nor did dropout rates budge after the curriculum overhaul.[60]

Carolina Arteaga, an economist at the University of California, Los Angeles, seized on this reform as the perfect opportunity to study whether the human capital theory of degree value holds true. She compared the postgraduation wages before and after the reforms of economics and business graduates at Los Andes and other top-10 Colombian universities that didn't change their degree requirements. Her study, published in 2017 in the *Journal of Public Economics*, found that the wages of economics graduates from Los Andes dropped by 16 percent and that the wages of business graduates dropped by 13 percent. In addition, she surveyed employers and found that the reduction in mandatory courses may have left job candidates with less knowledge in important content areas for the jobs they were seeking. As a result, she found, the course content changes led to a 17 percentage point reduction in the likelihood of graduates of Los Andes being hired. Arteaga concluded that these results don't rule out some function for signaling, but they indicate that human capital "plays an important role" in determining wages.[61]

In fact, the power of human capital plays such a decisive role in college value that common measures of "underemployment" may be much less persuasive than they first seem. Large-scale data analytics firms like Emsi Burning Glass, now Lightcast, commonly measure underemployment by using occupational codes created by the government and determining whether an individual with a bachelor's degree works in an occupation that doesn't typically require that credential. Under this definition, that individual is underemployed. The same logic is used in much popular commentary to suggest that college was likely a waste of time and money for the significant number of recent graduates who take jobs that don't require degrees.

Yet these broad-brush measures do not establish much that is definitive about the value of degrees, however often they are used as debating points. Whether a job requires a bachelor's degree doesn't demonstrate whether the broad and targeted skills often held by college graduates might make an individual perform that role more effectively. A degree holder who works as a caterer or takes over the family dry-cleaning business would be formally described as underemployed, Katz observes, but might be using his or her skills very effectively to improve the success of the business. A contractor working in the building trades doesn't require a college degree. But if that person has a bachelor's degree, has learned some art and design, and can communicate particularly well with high-income households, he or she may secure important business and "get a very high return," Katz adds. This doesn't mean a degree is a guarantee against getting stuck in a career and salary rut. However, it's a mistake to deploy the simple metric of a particular job's formal requirements to settle on the notion that underemployment suggests that college is not worthwhile.

Still, the alleged proliferation of college graduates working in bartender or barista jobs that don't require degrees has frequently been portrayed as a sure sign that college and its financial benefits are overrated. In a *New Republic* essay dissecting misleading media accounts, writer and education analyst Kevin Carey pointed out, first, that college grads cited as poster children for underemployment often progressed to careers that made good use of their education. Even more decisively, he showed how widely discussed accounts like *The Overeducated American*, which predicted that too many degrees would further lower wages for college graduates, turned out to be mistaken. In fact, Carey wrote, after the book was published, and as the narrative of underemployed graduates with credentials of dubious value continued to circulate,

the labor market was embarking on what turned into a decades-long run-up in the value of college degrees. Students continued to matriculate in record numbers. The percent of adults with a bachelor's degree passed 20 percent in the 1980s, 25 percent in the 1990s, and stands just below 30 percent today. Yet despite the increase in supply, the price that employers were willing to pay for college graduates went *up*, not down. The inflation-adjusted median wage of bachelor's degree holders increased by 34 percent from 1983 to 2008. (The earnings for high school dropouts, on the other hand, fell by 2 percent during the same time.)[62]

The exact magnitude and trajectory of economic returns to college is not written in stone, of course. The college earnings premium has flattened in recent years. Moreover, after the Covid-19 pandemic a tighter labor market led to rising wages for low-wage jobs, a compression of the wage distribution, and a fall in the college wage premium, according to an analysis by economists David Autor of MIT and Arindrajit Dube and Annie McGrew of the University of Massachusetts, Amherst.[63] Nevertheless, the long-standing trend remains unmistakable: enormous evidence shows that college degrees, including two-year associate credentials and four-year bachelor's degrees, provide an excellent mixture of broad and targeted skills that are rewarded in the career marketplace.

Nevertheless, it remains true that just over half of all Americans don't have degrees. In 2021, 37.9 percent of US adults age twenty-five years or older had completed a bachelor's degree or higher.[64] The percentage was higher among younger cohorts of adults: 41.6 percent of thirty-five- to fifty-four-year-olds had a bachelor's or above, compared to 33.2 percent of adults aged fifty-five and older.[65] An additional 10.5 percent of adults held associate degrees in 2021, bringing the national total of degree completion to 48.4 percent. The United States, like other countries, would be well served by a significant increase in the percentage of bachelor's or associate degree completers. Bringing the total to 60 percent, which was the Obama administration's 2020 goal, similar to the broader credential completion goal advanced by the influential Lumina Foundation, would represent huge progress toward greater economic prosperity and mobility. Yet it would still leave an enormous number of people in need of alternatives to the traditional college route. The next chapter will address the enormous demand for short-term, affordable credentials; why economic changes make more postsecondary education desirable for all kinds of people; and how individuals can determine which alternative credentials and programs have the characteristics most likely to lead to career advancement.

Chapter 3

Alternative Credentials

After growing up in the Adams Morgan neighborhood of Washington, DC, and graduating from Bell Multicultural High School in 2013, Jeffrey Diaz Vega says going to college "was kind of like a downfall for me." He had earned good grades in school and considered going directly to the University of Maryland. But the tuition bill "kind of threw me off a bit." His parents are immigrants from Guatemala. His father worked as a security guard at Johns Hopkins University, and his mother runs a day-care center. He decided to begin at Montgomery College, a community college in the nearby suburbs, to save money for two years before transferring to Maryland.[1]

It didn't go well. He didn't feel well prepared—in retrospect he feels that the teaching wasn't strong in his high school and that he received high marks because of low expectations. He ended up failing calculus and leaving Montgomery College. Struggling in class felt like a waste of money, all the more so because he faced out-of-pocket costs despite receiving a federal Pell grant. He wasn't aware of a DC tuition assistance program that would have given him in-state tuition at Montgomery College. In the years that followed, he drifted, taking and then leaving an intern position at the National Education Association, being unemployed, and ultimately working at his mother's day-care center until he lost his job when the pandemic began.

Eventually, Diaz Vega realized it was time to overcome self-doubt and start acquiring the skills he would need to compete with others who had more work experience and more credentials: "I decided, 'Hey, I need to get my life together. I need to see if can become a professional.'" A high school friend who works in software development for mortgage giant Fannie Mae told him about a program that trained interns who were often eventually hired full-time despite not having college degrees. He soon signed up for Year Up, a nonprofit that provides six months of intensive training in hard and soft skills, followed by a guaranteed six-month internship placement. Although Diaz Vega had eventually gone back to Montgomery College, earning his associate degree in 2021—eight years after completing high school—he saw Year Up as a vital stepping stone. "I needed those skills to become career ready," he says.

Speaking to a visitor in the office space Year Up shares with several nonprofits on Capitol Hill, where he and the other young adults attending a regular check-in session all wear the business attire customary for program participants, Diaz Vega says the classes he began with in data analytics, coding, and fundamentals of Excel included a good deal of review for him because of his previous studies. But training in professional skills like how to present his experience confidently in job interviews, and the need for a concise résumé (he trimmed his down from three pages), was invaluable. At age twenty-six, he was the oldest in his Year Up cohort and had never previously had a formal job interview. He was impressed when representatives from Amazon, Facebook, and Exxon came to meet his trainee group. After completing his six-month placement at Capco, a management and technology consulting firm, he was "converted"—the Year Up term for being hired full time after an internship. With two years of college under his belt, eventually he'd like to get his bachelor's degree as well.

Year Up was created in 2000 by a former Wall Street analyst and Bowdoin College graduate, Gerald Chertavian. Through the Big Brother program, he had worked in the 1980s with David Heredia, a ten-year-old boy from the Dominican Republic who lived in a public housing development on the Lower East Side of New York City at the height of the crack cocaine and AIDS epidemic. It became clear to Chertavian after spending many Saturdays with Heredia that he had enormous potential, ambition, and skills. But he was held back by a combination of poverty, skin color, living in a bad neighborhood, and attending school in a troubled system. "It felt like a tremendous waste of human capital in a country where we have no one to waste," Chertavian said in a podcast interview.[2]

The workforce development nonprofit takes young adults—typically "opportunity youth" between eighteen and twenty-nine with little or no income—and provides hard and soft skills training followed by an internship, usually with a Fortune 500 company. Although the initial training phase usually lasts six months, Year Up is experimenting with shorter, accelerated formats. Most participants enter the program without postsecondary credentials, though students often enroll in a community college while participating. Year Up provides a modest stipend, because some kind of income stream is key for low-income participants. The program has become a leading source of low-income young adults who are hired into Fortune 500 jobs. Chertavian believes the internships are crucial to make that possible. "For the employer, it's an opportunity to try someone out before you hire them," he said.[3] "And as a result of that, our young adults are able to be seen in ways that often without that four-year degree, it would be impossible for them to be seen in these types of career paths." Once successfully placed, program completers earn an average annual starting salary of $44,000.[4]

Popularity and Pitfalls

It's an attractive scenario for many young people. For all the benefits that accrue to earning traditional two- and four-year degrees, large populations of learners need something different. That desire may be based on their immediate priorities (earning money for themselves and their families, lack of interest or aptitude for more classroom time, a desire for immediate hands-on work experience), difficulty persisting to a degree after enrolling, or some combination of these factors.

Yet effective, career-focused education and training that equips people with skills that meet market needs can be much harder to find than it should be. Tailored, shorter-term, skills-based programs and credentials in everything from digital marketing to graphic design should be widely accessible, simple to acquire and reacquire during a person's lifetime to meet changing needs. They should also be available to supplement a learner's existing degree with immediately marketable skills. And whenever possible, they should be possible to combine, over time, into full credentials so individuals seeking career preparation are not required to choose between targeted and broader skills but can be ready to develop both.

There are certainly plenty of credentials out there measured by sheer numbers. A clear-eyed look at the evidence, however, suggests huge variations in the quality and payoff of these alternatives. Too many short-term programs don't significantly boost earnings or career prospects and risk becoming a second-class route disproportionately pursued by low-income African American and Latino learners. Others, however, have a demonstrated ability to promote strong job outcomes, particularly when sponsoring institutions have strong connections to employers and training is clearly aligned to labor market needs and to a career ladder beyond the first job. Quality control and clear information and guidance is vital to help learners navigate the more than one million credentials,[5] plus other training pathways, now available in the United States. They need help figuring out how to separate the wheat from the chaff.

In the United States and around the world, opinion surveys show an emphatic and growing interest in short-term, career-focused credentials, accompanied by deep concern about the growing cost of college degrees and declining confidence in their value. This was true before the Covid-19 pandemic. In October 2019, for example, the publishing giant Pearson released a nineteen-country public opinion survey that found 68 percent of the more than eleven thousand respondents agreed that a credential from a vocational college or trade school was more likely to lead to a good job with strong career prospects than was a university degree.

The online survey drew responses from Argentina, Australia, Brazil, Canada, China, Colombia, Egypt, France, Germany, India, Italy, Mexico, Saudi Arabia, Spain, South Africa, Turkey, the United Arab Emirates, the United Kingdom, and the United States. Many agreed that older adults would need to continue upgrading their skills, and the largest share said they would do this through short-term programs like boot camps or certificates. In the United States, Australia, Canada, Brazil, China, and the Middle East, half as many people or fewer said that they would upskill through college or university training programs.[6]

After the coronavirus pandemic arrived, public preference for short-term credentials grew even stronger, from microcredentials and industry certifications to online certificates. As Paul Fain reported in *Inside Higher Ed*, interest in skills-based, online credentials with a strong career connection was particularly strong among the lower-income and minority adults that four-year colleges "often have struggled to attract and graduate." Fain reports that the credit rating firm Moody's projected in August 2020 that short-term credentials, while just 10 percent of overall enrollment in 2018, would continue to be the fastest-growing part of the higher education market.[7]

A series of surveys conducted by Strada Education Network at that time found a much stronger preference for skills training and nondegree credentials, at 37 percent and 25 percent, among the one in five Americans who planned to enroll in an education program in the coming six months.

Many fewer intended to enroll in bachelor's degree programs (16 percent) or associate degree programs (12 percent).[8]

These preferences were accelerated by the economic dislocation and uncertainty that accompanied the pandemic, but they were already well established in people's actual behavior. According to the think tank New America, one in four American workers has some kind of a nondegree credential—a certificate or license, for example. Fully half of undergraduate credentials as of 2015 were at the sub-baccalaureate level, while the number of short-term certificates awarded by college mushroomed by 151 percent from 2000 to 2010.[9]

For all the growth in their prevalence and popularity, however, short-term credentials have drawn significant scrutiny from observers who query whether they are delivering on promised outcomes and thus whether they provide a reasonable return on investment. That's particularly concerning for analysts who observe that racial and ethnic minorities (as well as women and older adults) are disproportionately likely to enroll in short-term programs.

"The movement toward increased racial tracking in higher education seems to be gathering new momentum, with a growing emphasis on short-term training and sub-baccalaureate awards," wrote Anthony Carnevale, director of Georgetown University's Center on Education and the Workforce, in an article published six months into the Covid-19 pandemic, entitled "White Flight to the Bachelor's Degree." While there's nothing wrong with short-term programs that lead to well-paying jobs, he wrote, the "surest gateway to economic and social progress" remains the bachelor's degree. "We must guard against the mindset that short-term training and sub-baccalaureate awards are good enough for the least advantaged among us."[10]

In a similar vein, but still more emphatically, New America warned that variations in return on investment for different kinds of credentials should raise alarm bells for policy makers. If sub-baccalaureate credentials have labor market value substantially worse than bachelor's degrees, Monique Ositelu argued in a March 2021 report, that reinforces "growing concern about the inevitable, continued stratification of higher education attainment, in which our most vulnerable students earn nondegree credentials that tend to be valueless towards social and economic mobility."[11] The short-term credentials often held by women or by workers in female-dominated occupations led to "substantially" lower earnings, according to New America, while Latino workers with certificates, and especially African Americans, had lower earnings than white workers with certificates.[12]

New America's director of higher education, Amy Laitinen, is particularly wary of very short-term programs that haven't traditionally been eligible for Pell grant funding but whose students might qualify under proposed reforms for so-called short-term Pell. Just as four-year degrees provide significantly higher average economic returns than do two-year degrees, six-month or one-year certificate programs offer better chances of some kind of earnings boost than courses that last as little as eight weeks. "It's just wishful thinking," Laitinen says. "It's just like everyone wants five-minute abs, but five-minute abs aren't a thing."[13]

As discussed in the previous chapter, given the huge variety of bachelor's degree programs, any analysis of their value and effectiveness necessarily requires caveats about economic returns representing averages and variations across fields of study. For shorter-term, nondegree credentials with still fewer shared characteristics, data that permit conclusions about results are even harder to obtain and more variable. Program length can vary from weeks to months to years. Some colleges offer credit for certificates, often under the rubric of career and technical education, or CTE. Many employers provide noncredit programs. A range of courses lead to industry-recognized credentials.

What's more, notes Di Xu, associate professor at the University of California, Irvine, noncredit students and programs aren't usually included in state and national postsecondary data collection. That means limited information about program types and outcomes for a large number of students. These students, often working adults who are disproportionately from low-income backgrounds, have little access to financial aid, including Pell grants targeted at students in credit-bearing programs. Nor do they receive much advising, whether on careers or making the transition to credit-bearing programs. "Without those services," Xu says, "or if the services or support are limited, students are likely to struggle more."[14]

An enormous number of government, nonprofit, and business efforts have attempted to create effective education and training routes outside the well-known path to college. But in recent decades, despite significant spending on workforce development programs through federal, state, and local initiatives, results have often been disappointing. Under the Workforce Innovation and Opportunity Act (WIOA) and its predecessors, federal dollars typically filtered down to the local level,

where workforce boards often spent them on activities rang-
ing from job fairs to job shadowing to structured internships
and nascent forms of work-based learning. The historical bar
for a program's success was whether those who completed
went on to employment in any kind of job. Providing new
training or specialized preparation might lead someone to
a new employer, but those program activities were not very
effective in boosting earnings. Across dozens of federal
programs, summary research found only modest positive
impacts for adult men and women and no impact at all for
out-of-school youth.[15]

What Works

However, a group of programs that includes Year Up have led
to strong outcomes. Garrett Warfield, the nonprofit's chief research officer, cites a set of shared characteristics that have led
his and similar sectoral employment programs, such as Per
Scholas, to impressive earnings for many graduates. The first,
perhaps unsurprising but vital for near-term results, is that
training needs to match where the strongest demand lies in
the labor market. Another is the need to recognize the significant opportunity costs for participants by providing compen-
sating benefits. Unlike many postsecondary programs, Year
Up is free to participants and provides a modest stipend, both
of which help offset the loss of earnings during the first six
months.

The most decisive selling point is the built-in, paid internship during the second half of the year, together with the pos-
sibility that the guaranteed internship will turn into a paid job.

"If there were one Jenga piece in the tower that I wouldn't want to pull out, that would be it," Warfield told me when we spoke in October 2021.[16] "It's a guaranteed opportunity to walk through that door and prove your worth to the employer." To attract participants, he says, "instead of just selling the internship seat, you pitch the job afterwards."

The pipeline approach appeals to employers as well. Bank of America, for example, has a goal of hiring ten thousand disconnected young adults and has exceeded its targets through partnerships with programs that include Year Up. Other corporations, including J. P. Morgan Chase, Facebook, and Apple, are eager to work with talent providers to bring in a diverse candidate pool. For jobs that don't necessarily require a college degree, companies see huge appeal in targeted training geared to furnishing employees who can "plug and play" into needed roles. The comfort of testing out candidates during an internship adds to the appeal.

While Year Up participants may not hold a bachelor's degree when they enter the program, the organization certainly doesn't position itself in opposition to degrees. Participants are often simultaneously enrolled in community college classes. Some, like Diaz Vega with his two years of college under his belt, eventually plan to earn bachelor's degrees as well. But in the near term they can develop valuable skills, build work experience, and embark on real career paths. They can also earn respectable wages that provide necessary financial stability should they pursue further education.

The set of programs with which Year Up is usually grouped are known as sectoral training programs. The term refers to initiatives that "train job seekers for high quality employment, or employment in specific industries considered to have strong labor demand and opportunities," in the words of a report from the Abdul Latif Jameel Poverty Action Lab (J-PAL) at the Massachusetts Institute of Technology.[17] These programs show promise in leading to better-paying jobs for workers, usually lacking college degrees, who face employment challenges, Samuel Lee and Caroline Garau of J-PAL note in their summary of a *Journal of Labor Economics* analysis by Lawrence Katz and three coauthors.[18] The difficulties these workers face have "helped drive the expansion in US educational wage differences and overall wage inequality," the analysis notes.

With a focus on in-demand occupations in commonly targeted sectors—health care, information technology, manufacturing, and financial services—the programs studied yielded significantly higher earnings in the year following completion of training. The review of results from four randomized evaluations of nine sectoral employment programs included Project QUEST; Year Up; Jewish Vocational Service—Boston; the Wisconsin Regional Training Partnership; Per Scholas; and several other providers that implemented a model called Work Advance. Earnings gains persisted in longer-term follow-up and, according to the J-PAL summary, were "among the largest found in evaluations of US training and employment services programs."[19] Gains weren't driven by higher employment rates or more hours worked, but from more participants working in better-paying jobs. The analysis used randomized evaluations, widely viewed as a gold-standard research design because it divides a group of similar people into two groups and then analyzes a program's impact on the group whose members are randomly assigned to participate.

In addition to targeting in-demand skills in industries with higher-paying jobs, effective programs shared several other common characteristics. Those include upfront screening in core math and literacy skills as well as vital career skills such as critical thinking, time management, and conflict resolution. A broad range of additional supports beyond the content of the training are key: those might include help with interview preparation and résumé polishing, but also, crucially, assistance finding job openings and building relationships with employers. Getting candidates ready for a particular sector often includes training that leads to widely recognized certifications and credentials in fields like nursing and computer repair, the J-PAL report notes.

The Last Mile Problem

One useful term for organizations like Year Up is "intermediaries." These can take many forms, from nonprofits to government-led efforts to business-backed groups. What they have in common is an ability to connect sectors that don't always speak the same language or make a priority of communicating their needs to other partners. Education investor and author Ryan Craig, cofounder of University Ventures and managing partner of a successor firm, Achieve Partners, says intermediaries are particularly vital for building bridges between education providers and employers. "Academic institutions are not employment oriented enough; they're not connected enough to understand or even care what these [in-demand] skills are." Nor are employers well positioned to solve their talent needs directly, given their multiple competing priorities in running their businesses. That's why there are eleven million unfilled jobs in the US economy, Ryan told me in March 2022—and why he's convinced emerging intermediaries will fill the gap.[20]

Craig sees a key role for what he calls "last mile" providers, who can reduce or remove hiring frictions for both job seekers and employers. On the job seekers' side, those frictions include the time and cost required for training and the uncertainty of an employment outcome. Employers face the risks of hiring unproven candidates. Craig's firm invested in service providers such as Revature, a software developer staffing firm, and more recently Optimum Healthcare IT, which trains analysts certified in a patient record system used by around 70 percent of large US hospital systems. By the time a hospital has finished the project for which it hired Optimum to provide trained analysts, those workers can be hired as the hospital's own employees.

Craig calls this model "talent as a service." It has a lot in common with traditional apprenticeships. And although those paid-training-and-work-experience programs have never been common in the United States outside skilled trades like plumbing and electrical, Craig recently joined longtime apprenticeship advocate Robert Lerman of the Urban Institute to launch Apprenticeships for America. The nonprofit hopes to dramatically expand apprenticeships and make what Craig terms "hire, train, deploy" programs, already oversubscribed, much easier to access.

Making more "last mile" programs easy to reach doesn't mean there should be less postsecondary education. Instead,

Craig would like a "radical restaging" of how education and training is "consumed" by students—from an all-you-can-eat-in-one-sitting model to pathways that give people what they need, when they need it. He readily acknowledges that many people will need to develop additional broad skills, including problem solving, critical thinking, and communication skills. But he's convinced there will need to be additional pathways, less expensive and time-consuming than traditional degrees, and likely online, to help people acquire those key career building blocks. Those unbundled options, he says, "don't exist yet."

Decisions, Decisions

For anybody who wants to choose among the enormous number of nondegree credentials that exist already, making a wise decision isn't easy. The United States has no equivalent of the national qualifications framework that exists in some countries to set forth how different education and training options meet specific career requirements. On both the employer side and the higher education side, the US system is highly decentralized. That makes navigating everything from badges and microcredentials to certificates extremely challenging—all the more so because of the more than one million unique credentials now offered in the United States, according to the nonprofit Credential Engine.[21]

Just developing a common vocabulary and set of definitions would be a good start, which is why analysts like Holly Zanville of George Washington University have launched efforts to forge agreement on shared terminology. More widely understood language would in turn make possible the more far-reaching goal of creating a system that recognizes learning as it occurs, in smaller units than the two- and four-year degrees that a little more than half of all Americans do not currently possess. Zanville and her collaborators Nan Travers, director of the Center for Leadership in Credentialing Learning at SUNY Empire State College, and Larry Good, president and CEO of the Corporation for a Skilled Workforce, write that "competing life circumstances"—notably work and family obligations—often make completion of time-consuming traditional degrees "unachievable" for many students.[22]

The thirty-nine million Americans who have "some college, no degree"[23] typically don't see the learning they've achieved and the credits they have earned bundled together into a recognizable credential. That kind of discrete measure of knowledge and skills could be recognized and valued in the labor market, whether to get a job or earn a promotion. Thus, Zanville and colleagues are promoting a "Credential as You Go" approach, with funding from Lumina Foundation. "We're prototyping incremental credentials," Zanville said in an interview.[24]

Continuing efforts to create clearer pathways for people with qualifications that fall outside the baccalaureate or associate degree certainly hold promise for people who have no immediate plans to pursue conventional postsecondary education. The same is true for the millions who had hoped to complete degrees but whose efforts were derailed. In the very tight labor market that followed the worst of the Covid pandemic, a more flexible approach to required credentials became a necessity for many employers. That was all the more true when high demand for skilled labor coincided with a desire to hire a more racially and socioeconomically diverse workforce.

The Mix and Match Approach

In addition, however, a third group has turned out to be a heavy consumer of nondegree credentials: those who already hold degrees and are seeking to supplement their original field of study with a different or more targeted specialty that may add meaningfully to their skill set, sometimes with a new set of job opportunities in mind.

Case in point: The soaring popularity of coding boot camps along with the growth of the tech economy. A 2020 survey of three thousand alumni of these short-term programs teaching marketable computer programming skills found that 74 percent already held college degrees.[25] That pattern is also reflected in the enrollment boom in short-term credential programs during the Covid-19 pandemic. Much of the growth in momentum took place in professional development credentials, with college graduates making up many of those enrolling. "They're people who are topping up—who are doing continuing education, in essence," says Sean Gallagher, founder and executive director of Northeastern University's Center for the Future of Higher Education and Talent Strategy.[26] The same was true for the vast majority of the millions of students who enrolled in MOOCs—Massive Open Online Courses—when they surged in popularity in 2012, which the *New York Times* called "the year of the MOOC."[27]

There's good reason to believe that combining full college degrees with targeted workforce skills leads to higher satisfaction among those who earned this combination of credentials. As the 2021 survey by Strada Education Network and Gallup discussed in chapter 1 found, adults with both a college degree and a nondegree credential were more likely than those with just a degree to report that they considered their education worth the cost, that it made them attractive job candidates, and that it helped them achieve their goals.[28]

This increased student satisfaction helped motivate a pilot program by the University of Texas system that aims to provide skills-based microcredentials in fields like data analysis to students in majors that have traditionally led to jobs with the lowest salaries, according to coverage in the *Hechinger Report*. Those include theater, studio art, creative writing, psychology, and anthropology, for which the typical annual median salary for graduates a year out of college is $30,000 or less. The hope is to take the kinds of practical offerings more commonly associated with community colleges and embed them into the curriculum of four-year colleges. Starting in 2022, the eight participating colleges in the giant UT system plan to provide direct workforce skills in conjunction with less lucrative academic majors to about thirty-seven hundred undergraduates and eventually, if the efforts prove successful, to many more.[29]

To be sure, there is no guarantee that this approach will improve postgraduation salaries. In the Strada and Gallup survey, higher satisfaction was not accompanied by higher reported earnings among adults with both a bachelor's degree and a nondegree credential.[30] (Nor are starting salaries necessarily high in many other majors, the *Hechinger Report* notes, from environmental science and biochemistry at UT El Paso to cognition and neuroscience at UT Dallas.) Still, campuses taking part in the pilot will work closely with local workforce leaders in an effort to ensure that participants graduate with both broad and targeted skills that improve their chances of finding good jobs in the regional economy.

Whether through this kind of explicit attention to add-on career skills, or through the built-in combination in many degree programs of broad academic competencies with vocational skills in fields like accounting or nursing, a college degree can often provide a useful mix of the skills needed to launch and sustain a career. But for many people who have already earned a degree in one field, returning to school for a short-term, career-focused credential in a different area often holds significant appeal.

Some traditional bastions of the liberal arts have taken notice. Sacred Heart University, in Fairfield, Connecticut, for example, is capitalizing on students' desire to combine academics with practical preparation by offering new certificate programs in fields from mammography and ultrasound to brewing science. "We don't want to lose the richness of the liberal arts," Sacred Heart president John Petillo told the *Hechinger Report*. "At the same time, we want to prepare you for life out there." One survey found that Americans are four times more likely to say they would hire an English major with a cybersecurity credential than an English major without one.[31]

When community colleges deliver on their promise of working closely with employers to assess and meet their talent needs, the resulting short-term, practical credentials can be extremely appealing to students from a range of backgrounds. At the Community College of Rhode Island, former high school classics teacher John Tebow enrolled in CCRI's Fast Track to CNC Manufacturing program. An advanced manufacturing "boot camp," the nineteen-week program prepares students for well-paid jobs in the state's fast-growing manufacturing sector.

Originally from Burrillville, Rhode Island, the son of a kindergarten teacher and an accountant, Tebow earned a classics degree from the University of Rhode Island in 1997 followed by a master's in teaching at Tufts University. He landed a job teaching Latin at a high school just outside Syracuse, New York. But after four years he lost his job when the program was dropped, and he had trouble finding another teaching position. He moved back to Rhode Island and took a job in a Frito Lay warehouse, in roles that included filling in as a supervisor and crane monitor. "I needed to make money," he said in an interview. "It was never a job that I really enjoyed." He ended up staying for thirteen years but finally decided to leave when he was passed over for a promotion he felt he deserved. "I had pretty much maxed out," he adds.[32]

Before long, Tebow saw an ad for the CCRI program, which offered free classes—costs are subsidized by Polaris MEP, a statewide nonprofit working to grow Rhode Island's manufacturing industry—as well as a small stipend to cover books and other expenses. Without that kind of support, he wouldn't have been able to take several months off work to make a career change. Good with his hands and eager to get practical experience, John took several subjects simultaneously, learning to run a lathe and milling machine in a machine shop with a small classroom off to the side where he studied things like print reading and dimensioning. After completing his coursework and earning a certificate, he quickly found several different jobs, has completed additional classes that can count toward an associate degree, and is earning a little over $50,000—an improvement over his warehouse job.

Tebow's background may be unconventional for a community college career changer, but in a sense there isn't a single typology of a typical student at an institution like CCRI. What many have in common, particularly in nondegree programs that offer a relatively short path to a better job, is the desire for extremely clear connections between what they study and new job opportunities.

Terris Gonsalves Wallace grew up poor in Providence and drifted after high school. He'd been a track star as a teenager and had notions of a future in everything from engineering and auto repair to finance. But although he graduated on time, he feels he was labeled "the bad kid" and says nobody talked to him about college possibilities.[33] He eventually started working at a Banana Republic store and later became a bartender before losing his job during the pandemic. During this period, he took his first CCRI class in college writing, then received an email telling him about a free Securities Industry Essentials (SIE) training course at the college. It covers topics from basic economic theory to equity and debt securities, plus investment strategies and industry regulations. The sixty-hour program leads to a national SIE exam that prepares students for careers in the financial securities industry.

Wallace, now thirty-three, passed the exam on his third attempt and has since passed the tough Series 7 and Series 6 exams that are standard industry requirements. He's working for Fidelity in a client services position and is interviewing for a promotion to an investment adviser role working with high net worth individuals. He also continues to take general education classes at CCRI and plans to transfer to the University of Rhode Island to major in engineering.[34] He has received education benefits and scheduling accommodations from Fidelity to support him in continuing his college classes. At CCRI, he particularly appreciates receiving guidance about how to channel his abilities into specific classroom and career pathways. "You want to go do something you're going to enjoy, but you also want to have useful skills," he says. "So getting an education is the best tool that you can have on your side."

The classes Wallace took exemplify the workforce partnerships CCRI has created to ensure that faculty and the offerings they provide stay up to date with fast-moving industry needs. "We bring together industry and faculty to build out programming," says Tekla Moquin, CCRI's former associate vice president for workforce partnerships, who points to the dozen or so new one-year certificate programs the college has created in the past couple of years.[35]

Programs with practical career applications are very appealing to working adults who may be self-conscious about having been poor students in high school, or who tried college and didn't persist, so are reluctant to enter a formal college setting. Employer demand and placement assistance ensure that the classes have good return on investment in the near term. Simply put, "you're going to leave with the skills you need for a job," Moquin told me. The availability of stipends or scholarships means students can often get paid while they're taking classes, which adds significantly to the appeal.

Stackable Credentials

Workforce programs can also get students started on an academic path. Academic credit is a key part of the workforce education formula at CCRI and a growing number of other institutions. Short-term alternatives to traditional two- and four-year degrees are popular in part because time and money are precious commodities for working adults. Obtaining new skills while continuing to work holds huge appeal for many people. This notion of integrating learning and earning has increasingly influenced education and workforce strategy to emphasize multiple options for acquiring new skills in a way that fits into an individual's life and existing work and family responsibilities.

But what about the limitations of short-term credentials compared to degrees in boosting earnings and providing the broad skills useful for navigating careers? Despite the strengths of Year Up and other sectoral training programs, there's good reason for many learners to choose very carefully when picking short-term programs, and then to be on the lookout for the potential long-term benefits of a degree. A middle-ground approach that attempts to provide the best of both approaches has attracted growing interest: stackable credentials.

The idea behind this strategy is that working adults should be able to pursue short, career-focused training and courses, earning credits and developing skills over time as their schedules permit while they hold down jobs. Eventually, their credits and credentials can be "stacked" into full degrees that provide cumulative career improvements in the process of acquiring the broad skills likely to help their long-term career prospects.

One advocate of stackable credentials, Allison Salisbury of Guild Education, offers the example of how a worker she calls Arnold could benefit from a cascading series of courses and qualifications. He started his career doing tech support at a call center. He's able to double his salary, to $60,000 a year, after earning a short-term IT credential paid for by his firm's education benefits program. Later, he can apply his initial credits, plus skills learned on the job, toward an associate degree that allows him to become a front-end web designer. After marrying and starting a family, he eventually goes back to school again. His two-year degree counts toward his BA, reducing the time and money needed for that degree. And after a decade, these steady, incremental opportunities to get ahead put him into a software architect role making $200,000 annually.[36]

This stackable credential scenario isn't yet widespread—just 2 to 4 percent of workers hold these credentials, the majority of whom already held degrees when they earned a certificate, according to the Community College Research Center at Teachers College.[37] But it is gaining traction, thanks in part to organizations like the American Council on Education, which certifies military and corporate training for college credit. In Colorado, a statewide report on student success and workforce revitalization cited the success of a program run by the Mi Casa Resource Center, which works with the Community College of Aurora, Metropolitan State University of

Denver, and more than thirty Denver-area financial institutions.[38] It offers what it calls an "on-ramp" for jobs in the financial services industry. Participants, who are typically low-income Latinos, can work while they earn a certificate in banking, an associate degree in business, or a bachelor of science in banking. A range of permutations allow students to stack one credential into another while pausing to enter the workforce full-time if that's their preference.

In the same vein, Robert Morris University and the University of Pittsburgh Medical Center have created a partnership that lets UPMC employees take leadership training classes at reduced costs. They can take their classes online, a big draw for working adults, and can apply credits toward a Leadership and Organizational Change certificate offered by Robert Morris or to its Master of Science in Organizational Leadership degree. The idea, as described by then Robert Morris president Christopher B. Howard and Burning Glass Institute president Matt Sigelman, is to identify in-demand skills in a regional economy, then to create pathways for working learners to build up their qualifications to become more desirable and better-paid employees. They write: "That might involve a multi-step pathway in which a file clerk learns budgeting and administrative support to become a better-paid office assistant, then later earns a bachelor's degree in accounting or finance to become a budget analyst at a significantly higher salary."[39]

This kind of collaboration illustrates vividly why for many people a yes-or-not dichotomy between college or practical skills simply doesn't reflect the options most likely to propel them to more satisfying and financially rewarding careers.

Many alternative credentials allow learners to build job-specific skills, whether early in their careers or later in life as supplements to degrees and work experience that also develop key broad abilities. Finding jobs and building successful careers often require a third element, however, which the next chapter will discuss in detail: the professional networks without which numerous useful skills are, by themselves, not enough.

Chapter 4

Social Capital

When Mark Granovetter was a PhD student in the late 1960s, studying how white-collar men find new jobs, he zeroed in on social networks. He repeatedly ran into the same answer when he asked interview subjects whether the person who told them about their current job was a friend. "Over and over again, they would correct me and say 'No, no, he's only an acquaintance,'" says Granovetter, now a professor of sociology at Stanford.[1]

The idea, he explains, is that a job seeker's close friends usually know the same people and can share only already familiar information. From acquaintances, by contrast, "you're going to get new information, new ideas, new ways of thinking."

Granovetter's paper summarizing these conclusions, "The Strength of Weak Ties," was published in the *American Journal of Sociology* in 1973 and became one of the most cited articles in social science.[2] His research codified the value of networking for professional success. By focusing on networks beyond close friends, it also added a new twist to the old saw: "It's not what you know; it's who you know." As Granovetter would have it, it's actually who you know just a bit.

Nearly fifty years later, with a healthy assist from the force multiplier of computer technology, personal and professional networking shows every sign of thriving. But that's not true across the board. Low-income Americans, racial minorities, and first-generation college students frequently struggle. Even when they've checked all the career-readiness boxes by earning college degrees or other credentials, disadvantaged job seekers typically navigate their careers with the fewest networking advantages.

As a result, according to a 2021 study of Florida State University graduates in the *Journal of Applied Psychology*, first-generation students have a harder time getting the same quality jobs as their better-connected classmates with the same credentials. Having more "occupationally focused relationships" and help with résumé-writing and interview skills provides a big boost compared to "job seekers of lower social class who lack such networks," the authors wrote.[3]

Even job seekers from modest backgrounds who can build promising network connections need to know how to use those contacts effectively. But they aren't getting much guidance. Case in point: College students often hope to participate in career-building activities as undergraduates. But the job-related activities they actually participate in by the time they are seniors too seldom match what they expected when they were freshmen. In a recent analysis of survey responses from fifty-five thousand US college students at ninety-one institutions, the National Survey of Student Engagement and Strada Education Network found that 70 percent of first-year undergrads planned to network with alumni or professionals in the field. But by senior year only 27 percent had done so.[4]

And the gaps were worse for first-generation students. As seniors they were significantly less likely than their peers to have engaged in social-capital-building activities like networking with alumni or professionals (11 percentage points less), discussing career interests with faculty (12 points less), or interviewing or shadowing someone in a career field that interests them (10 points less).[5]

Networks as a Missing Piece of the Skills Puzzle

Why are these gaps so striking? College remains highly effective for acquiring both broad and targeted employability skills, and nothing about networking alters that truth. Nonetheless, our emphasis on education and skills in the past fifty years, while necessary and valuable, has too often come at the expense of helping young people build the networks they need to thrive professionally, particularly in an era when growing life expectancies will mean multiple career changes. Rachel Lipson, former director of Harvard University's Project on Workforce, says it bluntly: "We've overemphasized skills relative to networks."[6]

Despite Granovetter's striking findings, five decades later networking of any kind is either underemphasized or misunderstood in the field of career readiness. Instead, the headline remains education and skills, and the college degrees and other postsecondary credentials that document them. "We've entirely ignored this asset in how we've designed our higher education and workforce system," Julia Freeland Fisher, director of education at the Clayton Christensen Institute, told me recently. "We've designed it around the premise of learning, but the premise of connections has been either outright ignored or downplayed, because in polite company you don't talk about how who you know is part of how you get jobs."[7]

The networks that a focus on social capital provides can pay off in extremely concrete ways. That's one reason many leaders in the world of career preparation argue for ensuring that broad education and marketable skills need to be combined with explicit steps to connect learners to jobs. "Looking across all the research, I think skills are important, but I think we sometimes over-index on skills when access to a high-quality job opportunity can be just as important," according to Garrett Warfield, chief research officer at Year Up. He believes the linchpin of his program—the Jenga piece—is the guaranteed internships that allow Year Up participants to prove their worth to employers.[8]

The strikingly insular nature of massively popular platforms like Facebook and LinkedIn doesn't help. When it comes to the expanded web of relationships people need to get jobs and advance in their careers, those social networks "tend to simply amplify users' offline networks and tendencies, rather than forging new, different, or expanded networks," wrote Fisher in her 2018 book *Who You Know: Unlocking Innovations That Expand Students' Networks*.[9]

Indeed, most Facebook "friends" already know each other in the nonvirtual world. The Pew Research Center found that the average Facebook user already knows 93 percent of her "friends" in real life, Fisher adds. "There is little to suggest that networking sites have extended the reach of those people's networks to new people whom they might not otherwise meet," she wrote.[10] And that's no accident. "Facebook has been focused on helping you connect with people you already know," wrote founder Mark Zuckerberg in a May 2017 post, as reported by Fisher. His frank acknowledgment of the company's strategy significantly undercuts his next point—that it "might be just as important" to forge new connections.[11] In any case, the site's impact on career networking for young people is modest: 18 percent of Facebook's US users were aged between eighteen and twenty-four as of December 2022, according to Statista.[12]

Several years ago, Meg Garlinghouse, LinkedIn's vice president for social impact, began to notice that the people contacting her on LinkedIn seeking informational interviews were all advantaged white women with four-year college degrees. "They were kind of in my network," she recalls. "I was like 'Oh my God, I'm unintentionally helping the people who look just like me.'"[13]

Her experience reflects something LinkedIn discovered when it introduced a tool called InMaps for creating visual representations of a person's network. If a person's digital plot looks like a flower, it means most of that person's contacts are connected to different people. When the diagram looks like a hockey puck, as many did, it means most of those contacts already know a lot of the same people. That seems to undermine much of the point of networking: people outside that tight circle can't capitalize on the weak-tie connections that Granovetter showed are instrumental in catapulting people into new circles where they can find new opportunities.

The weak ties theory received compelling empirical support in 2022 in a study published in *Science* magazine by a LinkedIn researcher and colleagues at MIT, Harvard Business School, Stanford, and the National Bureau of Economic Research. The authors used data from over twenty million LinkedIn users over a five-year period, during which time two billion new ties and six hundred thousand new jobs were created. Using a randomized experiment in which different LinkedIn users got relatively stronger or weaker connection recommendations from the "People You May Know" feature, the researchers found that weak ties did in fact lead to a greater likelihood of "job transmission."[14] Another much-discussed 2022 study underscored a related advantage of networks that include dissimilar people, beginning early in life. Economist Raj Chetty and several colleagues wrote in *Nature* that poor children who have more affluent neighborhood friends—the researchers call this "economic connectedness"—have future incomes that are 20 percent higher because cross-class friendships are likely to foster opportunity.[15]

There's a strong case that even as many efforts to improve social capital are appropriately focused on people from economically disadvantaged backgrounds, networks matter far more than has been recognized for students and job seekers across the board.

Consider the much-discussed decline of social capital nationally—less connectedness, whether talking to neighbors or joining a local club—outlined by Robert Putnam in the landmark 1995 essay that eventually became his book *Bowling Alone*.[16] Add in the isolation and mental health woes associated with Covid-19, and it's not a surprise that building better career opportunities has suffered along with so much else. "The Pandemic Has Erased Entire Categories of Friendship," read the headline of an *Atlantic* article on the social and professional ramifications of eroding weak ties.[17]

That said, it's impossible to overstate the socioeconomic disparities that accentuate the social capital gap. LinkedIn's own research, for example, shows that a job seeker with a LinkedIn referral from a current employee is nine times more likely to get hired. Yet a member raised in a well-off zip code is three times as likely to have a robust network, with many connections from a range of places. Members who graduated from well-known colleges and had a first job at a top company are twice as likely to have strong networks.[18]

What Colleges Are Doing

The problem of unequal social capital has been recognized by "a very small number" of colleges and universities, according to the *Hechinger Report*, including the University of Toledo, California State University, Fullerton, and the University of California, Berkeley. They've launched a range of career-counseling classes, networking events, and mentoring programs for first-generation students.[19]

While four-year colleges and universities have a decidedly mixed record on helping students develop career-related connections, elite institutions that frequently attract well-networked undergraduates and give them focused attention are often singled out for their effectiveness in cultivating social capital. "Expensive four-year liberal arts degrees demonstrate the extent to which peers, alumni, professors, advisors, and career services officers create economic opportunity for students," concluded "Beyond Skills," a 2021 joint report from the SkillUp Coalition and Climb Hire. "They broker introductions, demystify and advise on the job search process, and share knowledge from similar experiences in their own career trajectories."[20]

Students from less affluent backgrounds often lack the networks of well-off undergraduates who have college-educated parents with professional credentials, according to Dana Hamdan, associate dean and executive director of the Career Development Center at Oberlin College. Students in the latter category "know how to ask for help, and help is usually no more than one degree of separation away," she wrote in an essay for *Inside Higher Ed*.[21] They "are already embedded in a thick social network that can help them launch after college."

In fact, they get an even earlier start by exploring careers and developing more connections when they secure internships and carefully chosen summer jobs. That's far rarer for less privileged students without someone at home to coach them on professional matters and with a practical need for jobs to pay for tuition. The result, Hamdan explains, is that those undergraduates don't know what questions to ask and end up without relevant work experience and internships. "For them, there is no thick and extensive social network— only social barriers that can't be easily overcome by learning to polish a résumé."

In response, Oberlin created its own cohort-based model for boosting social capital. The elite liberal arts college in Ohio designed its "Junior Practicum" with two stages. First, three hundred third-year students spend the month of September

on skill building and career readiness. Later, in keeping with
the needs of the pandemic era, they participate in remote
micro-internships. In the course of the program, organizers
address challenges like anxiety and imposter syndrome. Hamdan calls this part of "a thorough transformation of how we
prepare students for the professional world" following the
calls for racial justice that consumed the nation following
the murder of George Floyd in May 2020.

The broad networking disconnect has been noticed by private entrepreneurs as well. In 2014 three not-especially-wired
undergraduates at Michigan Technology University, frus-
trated with how few recruiters from companies outside the
Midwest came to their nonelite Upper Peninsula campus,
took matters into their own hands. Determined to democra-
tize access to information and opportunity, they launched
Handshake, a platform for professional networking and graduate recruitment. The startup grew quickly. Today the company
serves twelve million students and young alumni from fourteen hundred educational institutions. It works with more
than 650,000 companies, including all of the Fortune 500,
providing services that include building relationships, video
interviews, and online career fairs.[22]

As it grew, the company significantly expanded career networks for low-income students. Six years ago, about 20 percent
of undergraduates using Handshake were recipients of Pell
grants—well below the one-third or so of students nationally
awarded the need-based federal financial assistance. Today,
the figure has grown to 32 percent thanks to the company's
new partnerships with hundreds of community colleges and
historically Black colleges.[23] "We've realized that social capital

is still very core and very key to the career journey," says Handshake's chief education strategy officer, Christine Cruz-vergara. "For someone who doesn't have a lot of connections, this is a nonintimidating place where the barrier is lower for them to initiate a conversation." That's often with a weak tie, she adds—"someone who you don't know really well, not a close friend," such as a fellow student in the same major or a graduate of the same university.[24]

Nonprofits Helping Build Career Networks

Growing social capital has become a priority for a group of nonprofits that equip disadvantaged students to build broader and more effective networks. The organizations that work to cultivate social capital often use variations of the expression "know who" to capture the role of relationships in setting the stage for getting jobs, changing jobs, earning promotions, and acquiring the information needed for all three.

Beyond 12

For Oakland, California–based Beyond 12, the process starts with college access and completion. The organization provides personalized online coaching to first-generation and low-income college students using a mobile app and "near peers" with similar backgrounds. The goal is to show participants how to access the resources, relationships, and opportunities they need to succeed in college and then translate their degrees into meaningful employment.

Founder Alexandra Bernadotte, who came to the United States from Haiti as a young child, found her own path to an elite college almost by accident through the loosest of workforce networks. Her mother, a hospital phlebotomist, overheard a group of doctors in the emergency room talking about how good Dartmouth College is. She managed to send her daughter there. Ms. Bernadotte's own network has been a valuable part of her success. One of her Dartmouth friends, star TV showrunner Shonda Rhimes, now sits on her board.

Sitting in an Oakland coffee shop on a fall morning, Bernadotte described the "resource gaps" she faced as a high school student in inner-city Boston. The challenge began with relationships: "I didn't know who to go to for help—I did not." Even after making it to Dartmouth, thanks in part to her mother's attentiveness to the doctors' conversation at her hospital, Bernadotte struggled. She felt underprepared and found herself avoiding resources that might have been useful, such as meeting directly with professors or taking advantage of other academic assistance. "I thought going to professors' office hours or going to tutoring was a sign of weakness and a sign that I did not belong," she explains. "So I kept trying to do it on my own."[25]

With the help of a network that included some peers from similar backgrounds, and a particularly influential sociology professor, Deborah King, Bernadotte made it to graduation. She went on to a successful career in a series of for-profit and nonprofit organizations, earned a master's degree at Stanford University, became an entrepreneur in residence at New Schools Venture Fund, and in 2009 launched Beyond 12. The group's goal is to coach participants from low-income, first-generation backgrounds to access the resources, relationships, and opportunities they need to succeed in college and then translate their degrees into meaningful employment.

It also aims to take an "asset-based approach" to what students can bring to their college experience. Bernadotte herself came to see that she brought a valuable perspective to class discussions, "as annoying as it was to often be 'the voice of the Black person in America.'" She wants Beyond 12 participants to learn that experiences like working many hours in after-school jobs while in high school gives them both life skills and a point of view that their college classmates may lack.

A key part of the Beyond 12 model is to use recent graduates with similar life experience as "near-peer" coaches. One of the Bay Area coaches, Michelle Dew, grew up in rural Oklahoma before gaining admissions to Dartmouth. The daughter of a Cherokee father and a white mother, she describes herself as the only Black person in her "white-passing family." Growing up, "I didn't know what networking was, or the importance of networking," Dew said in an interview.[26] "That isn't something that was taught to me in high school, especially with my family background. That wasn't something that was ever emphasized." Her mother didn't attend college. Her father started, left school, and only finished fifteen years later. Many of her high school classmates went into professions and trades, becoming nurses, welders, and electricians.

Dew is doing her best to equip her students with the social capital she lacked when she arrived on campus as an over-whelmed first-year. She aims to show them that they can build a circle of support by communicating with professors, mentors, and academic advisers, along with making friends and finding meaningful activities. But it isn't easy. "They are very shy—shy isn't the right word; I would say intimidated," Dew says. "Fearful is another word." The students she works with are excited but often feel unprepared for the new world of college. Many, adds Dew, feel "a lot of imposter syndrome." Some lack strong study skills, or struggle to balance schoolwork with intense work schedules. When a challenge comes up, like being unsure about picking a major, or needing to get a financial aid hold lifted, students frequently feel isolated and that they don't belong. One of the best things coaching can accomplish, Dew says, is simply to help students understand that they aren't alone. Building trusting relationships with these students helps empower them to advocate for themselves.

Braven

The next step is getting students from disadvantaged backgrounds launched into strong first jobs. That's the mission of Chicago-based Braven, which works with university partners that include Rutgers University–Newark, National Louis University, and San Jose State University.[27] Braven combines a credit-bearing undergraduate course with coaching by volunteers from the professional workforce for small teams of five to eight students. Students learn teachable skills like writing cover letters and résumés, and practicing job interviews. At the same time, they are coached in forming networks, advocating for the value of their skills and credentials, and using referrals and informational interviews to secure internships and career-focused jobs.

Andrej Gjorgiev, twenty-four, signed up for Braven's career-preparation class as a criminal justice and psychology major at Rutgers–Newark. He learned how to seek the kind of connections he would have had trouble making on his own as the child of a construction worker and a night-shift lab technician who immigrated from Macedonia a decade ago. "A lot of the time, if you don't know people, it's hard to get outside of just your family," he said. "Braven gave me the idea of 'You should reach out to other people for help, and they are willing to help.'"[28]

The organization's founder, Aimée Eubanks Davis, grew up on Chicago's South Side before moving to a more affluent suburb. A former sixth-grade teacher in New Orleans, she entered the classroom as a Teach for America corps member following her graduation from Mount Holyoke College. She went on to hold several senior executive roles over thirteen years at the influential education reform group. The idea for creating a new organization devoted to career success for college graduates from low-income families came to her when she saw the struggles of her former students after they graduated from college the same year that Hurricane Katrina struck Louisiana. "I was seeing students come out of some of the top universities in the country and just simply not have the same quality of job that I would have assumed they would have received with their bachelor's degree," she told me when I interviewed her with cohost Andrew Hanson for the *Lessons Earned* podcast.[29]

Eubanks Davis became captivated by research showing that people's earnings in their first job out of college have a significant impact on their lifetime earnings trajectory. The pattern of less career-oriented first jobs and lower initial salaries for low-income, first-generation college graduates had lasting consequences for them. She created Braven to create a systematic program to address the problem.

As Braven collaborates with universities that serve many low-income students, a key part of its model comes from its partnerships with employers such as Deloitte, Prudential, and LinkedIn. It's a mutually beneficial arrangement. Employers welcome the prospect of diversifying their talent pools by recruiting well-prepared college graduates from disadvantaged backgrounds. Program participants value high-quality professional connections that help them put their abilities to good use. As Julia Freeland Fisher emphasizes, developing social capital is about much more than learning networking skills: it requires giving people *access* to networks. Eubanks Davis likes to say that she believes in teaching a person to fish—and also to stock the pond.

Braven's combination of activities has been particularly effective because of the guidance of a leadership coach who gives students a direct relationship with a professional that they often hadn't had before. When the program launched using that model, Eubanks Davis told me, "all of a sudden we were manufacturing social capital."

Braven was launched in 2013 and has grown slowly by design, mindful of the need to secure the right university partners. When the Covid-19 pandemic upended colleges and universities, together with the entire economy, the organization took some of its existing online materials to create a set of intense short-term models called the "Braven Booster."

Close to nine hundred students completed the program, adding significantly to the twenty-four hundred students across four universities the organization was serving in person. Interest in the organization has continued to grow; in 2021 it announced a new partnership with Spelman College, the historically Black women's college. The following year, Braven said it would add a second CUNY campus, City College of New York, as a partner.[30] It also launched a partnership with Northern Illinois University, using fully virtual programming, that aims to serve one thousand Northern Illinois students by its third year.[31] Other collaborations may be on the horizon.

In Newark, the Rutgers partnership with Braven has served as a catalyst to bring together multiple university and community goals. Corporate partners include Apple, insurance and financial services giant Prudential, and the audiobook and podcast company Audible—the latter two are headquartered in downtown Newark close to the Rutgers campus. Sitting in her office with a visitor and two Braven leaders, Rutgers–Newark president Nancy Cantor explained that her university's strategic plan is organized almost entirely around establishing the campus as an anchor institution that fosters social mobility and helps the substantial collaborations underway to make Newark thrive.

Cantor says students, and businesses looking to hire people with skills in fields like computer science, from diverse backgrounds, are well served by the mixture of preparation Braven provides, from internships and group work to capstone projects and mentoring relationships. Much of this work existed previously but was siloed. "What Braven does is bring it all together," she says. "Newark has a really unusual set of highly aware major corporations. The question is how to really get them the workforce they need. It's not that people aren't ready. It's how do we actually make those connections?" Braven plays a crucial role by getting "the people working in those corporations at the table with the students."

COOP Careers

Unfortunately, for too many low-income students college graduation continues to often mean underemployment. Farzana Chowdhury, whose parents run a newsstand in Brooklyn, immigrated to the United States from Bangladesh when she was seventeen. She graduated from Brooklyn College and considers her education well worth the time and money. Where it fell short was preparing her for next steps. "In college, we were constantly hustling—'Let me get this degree, let me get this class, let me get this credit, let me get this GPA.' But what happens after that?" she says. "Nobody preps you for interview skills. Nobody preps you for 'Hey, after you graduate, start applying for internships, start looking into jobs, start going into LinkedIn—fix your LinkedIn.'"[32] She got that help as a participant in social-capital-and-skills nonprofit COOP Careers. She later worked as program manager for the organization's data analytics track, and she recently started a job in digital marketing at Disney's New York office.

The elements Chowdhury felt were missing from her otherwise excellent Brooklyn College education are precisely those that COOP Careers was created to shore up. The organization collaborates with large, broad-access public institutions, notably the City University of New York (CUNY), San Francisco

State University, and the University of Illinois Chicago, and with major employers such as Google and Microsoft. It works with recent graduates who may be employed in one or more part-time jobs as coffee shop baristas or in retail sales, but who are seeking more lucrative employment with a promising career ladder. Its core belief: that network building, including relationship building and community building, is the key agent of change for getting a job.

Like Beyond 12, COOP uses a near-peer model in which it draws on graduates of its own program to serve as coaches, known as captains, to mentor participants. Part of its thinking is that building a strong community means low-income college graduates can help one another, and future rounds of participants, with accessing interviews and jobs. This kind of long-lasting professional network mitigates the assumption that rubbing shoulders with more affluent, often white, tech workers is required for getting ahead.

The program lasts five months, with three-hour sessions held in the evenings four nights per week to accommodate the work schedules of "COOPers." Part of the time is targeted at developing specific job-relevant skills. In a November 2021 session held via Zoom for a group of New York City participants who are mostly CUNY graduates, sixteen members of the data analytics track overseen by Chowdhury focused carefully on Python software exercises presented by a guest instructor from Microsoft. Two other COOP tracks offer training in digital marketing and tech sales.

Yet according to Markus Ward, COOP's managing director of development, it would be a mistake to view the cohort-based program primarily through the programmatic lens of job training. "We're probably the organization least convinced by the skills gap that you'll find—but we still like skills," he says. "It's just that we're overwhelmed with talking about skills," when earning credentials alone may not be enough to raise wages. Over time, he contends, navigating the labor market successfully hinges on personal referrals from other employees. "Skills don't necessarily protect you. Relationships are what protect you."[33]

Relationships were certainly a central part of what COOP founder Kalani Leifer acquired as an undergraduate at Stanford University: "That's literally what it was—it was a place to build deep, intimate relationships with peers over four years, 24/7." He's well aware that this "extremely rare and privileged experience," what he calls "marinating in social capital," makes up a significant part of the value of his degree.[34] And it's an experience not often shared by the kind of students he taught in his first job out of college at the Bronx high school where he spent two years as a history teacher through Teach for America.

After working as a McKinsey consultant and at Google, Leifer launched COOP Careers in 2014. His hope is that COOP's cohort-based approach will help its graduates avoid working in jobs that don't require a bachelor's degree, which is one frequent definition of underemployment. Among other things, that requires correcting the misconceptions of graduates who may think there's something wrong with them, that their difficulties succeeding in the economy stem from being broken in some way, and instead teaching them to value and convey to others their strengths. Being a shift manager at Starbucks, for example, may demonstrate a level of accountability and responsibility that other candidates don't offer.

Understanding that relationships unlock opportunity, including financial advancement, is another lesson Leifer wants COOP to teach. When working with early cohorts of participants, he liked to remind COOPers that they should be paying a lot of attention to their peers around the room. "These people are going to be important," he remembers saying. "And one of them is going to be the reason you get your first $50,000 job. But you don't know which one." By this math, each of ten peer relationships could be valued at an average of, say, $5,000. That might seem like an awful way to think of a human being and a friend, Leifer says, but this kind of assessment could be helpful if it leads people to be intentional about how they prioritize relationships.

Climb Hire

Bay Area–based Climb Hire takes a similar approach for working adults who may not have completed college, or even decided to start. It blends technical training for "new collar" jobs in Salesforce administration, financial services, or Google project management with networking events and coaching to build confidence, community, and white-collar professional relationships.

The organization's premise is that building networks to advance in the job market is as important for those who opt not to attend a two- or four-year college as it is for those with traditional academic credentials. Just as some college graduates without strong social capital face underemployment, many young people without postsecondary credentials and professional connections can easily get stuck in poorly paid and unfulfilling jobs. Social entrepreneur Nitzan Pelman launched Climb Hire to create a model for changing that.

The program uses a cohort model in which participants take 150 hours of online classes, divided between technical skills and developing social capital. Instruction is accompanied by peer-to-peer support and mentoring in small groups. The goal is to develop close connections between participants, mentors and alumni, and program staff, all of whom can link graduates to meaningful professional work.

Through its networking events, conducted virtually during the Covid-19 pandemic, Climb Hire is explicit about its central goal of relationship building. The idea of cultivating "homophily" drives the group's work. The word refers to people's desire to associate with those with whom they have something in common, because similarities and commonalities build trust. So it's vital to share personal stories to create connections with others.

Pelman is emphatic that skills by themselves simply won't fill many broader needs. In a recent discussion with Climb Hire's fifth cohort, she told the group that if they had signed up to build their technical skills, they'd be better off taking online courses through platforms like Coursera or LinkedIn Learning. Her goal is to build community and create the kind of relationships that will open doors "for your first job, and for your tenth job."[35] Indeed, just as four-year degrees provide broad skills that give graduates long-term flexibility to pursue a range of career options, Pelman and other social capital advocates see robust networks as a renewable resource that can help young people advance in their careers over time.[36]

Pelman's LinkedIn feed is full of accounts of "Climbers" who have taken what they've learned through the program to get ahead. In an interview near her home in the Berkeley hills, she tells the story of a participant who worked as a cook in the cafeteria of a Silicon Valley firm. Miguel Ruiz developed new skills through Climb Hire and now works at IBM making a $75,000 annual salary. He's also a fellow with the nonprofit, offering coaching and support to a group of five participants.

Climb Hire now has participants in the San Francisco Bay area, Los Angeles, Denver, and Minneapolis. In its "Beyond Skills" report with the SkillUp Coalition, it suggests that efforts to improve social capital will be required on a much larger scale. "At its core," the report says, "this is a story about how 'know-who'—relationships that can be leveraged into recommendations, referrals, and meaningful work experience—is the missing ingredient for workforce training and development in the United States."

Conclusion

As for networking giant LinkedIn, when it came to recognize that networks aren't distributed equally, it began to take steps to close the network gap. Garlinghouse helped introduce the "Plus One Pledge" that encourages LinkedIn members to do informational interviews with people outside their existing professional network, to mentor, and to introduce job seekers to friends or colleagues. More than 60 percent of the company's own employees took the pledge in its first year.[37]

Breaking into new networks will no doubt still be challenging for many people, even as these new tools develop and gain popularity. But it's encouraging that, for low-income students seeking to build career success with modest inherited networks, education and skills are increasingly recognized to be necessary but not sufficient. Social capital shouldn't have to play second fiddle any longer.

Chapter 5

Conclusion

THE EIGHT CAREER ARTS

What does it take to get ahead? This final chapter is intended as a recap and a look forward. I've distilled the main takeaways from the first four chapters into eight career arts. My goal is to give readers, including students, potential students, and those who want to support them, a handbook for career success in a changing world. In sum, these are a set of principles, recommended practices for how learners can best equip themselves for the future by acquiring a mixture of broad education, targeted skills, and social capital.

The Eight Career Arts

1. Go to college (yes, it's a good idea)
2. Find the best *kind* of college and program
3. Complete college
4. If pursuing nondegree options, purposefully build education, skills, and networks

5. Seek a both/and combination of broad and targeted skills

6. Take advantage of employer-funded education benefits

7. Find effective ways to build social capital

8. Prepare for the world as it is, not as you wish it were

The First Career Art:
Go to College (Yes, It's a Good Idea)

Public discussion about education after high school is often distorted by the claim that a movement promoting "college for all" is somehow forcing too many young people into a lockstep four-year undergraduate experience for which many are ill suited. The result, the argument goes, is that alternatives like apprenticeships, trade schools, or just moving directly into the workforce are both denigrated and not adequately developed, leaving anyone who opts against college feeling like a second-class citizen. This college-centric focus, according to this line of reasoning, sets up too many students for failure when a wider array of postgraduation options would help them obtain jobs and training more appropriate to their interests and abilities—and more suited for our workforce needs.

But the idea that a college-for-all juggernaut is crushing all alternatives in its path is largely a straw man. In any case, promoting college *readiness* to give more students a plausible shot at some kind of postsecondary education is undoubtedly worthwhile. History provides good reason to fear that late bloomers, or bright but disengaged students, or teens who school officials just don't see as college material, will be steered toward vocational tracks that typically don't offer the long-term promise and flexibility of traditional degrees.

The concern is all the more pressing when race and class are added to the discussion. As the nonprofit initiative Accelerate ED notes, two-thirds of today's jobs require education and training beyond high school, but just six in ten Black and Latino high school graduates enroll immediately in a postsecondary program after high school, compared to seven in ten of their white counterparts.[1] Degree completion gaps disaggregated by race, ethnicity, and class remain dismayingly large.

Yet skeptics continue to link these disappointing outcomes to the supposed college-for-all agenda and its fundamentally off-target assumptions. Their misguided critique undermines efforts to improve postsecondary attendance and completion rates for disadvantaged minorities. The critique is problematic in part because it is defeatist, suggesting that the goal of raising degree attainment for those groups may not be realistic or desirable. It also romanticizes nondegree alternatives.

Those alternatives may well be necessary or useful at times, and in any case the different paths individuals chose should be treated with respect. Still, whether it comes in the form of imagining an economy filled with happy, well-paid plumbers and welders, or decrying the "paper ceiling" that forestalls hiring minority job candidates with skills but without degrees, it seems patronizing to steer minority groups away from the degrees that are so widely understood, with good reason, to be extremely useful stepping stones to financial and career success.

Little wonder, then, that I have been struck repeatedly by the concerns of African American and Latino leaders—including Aimée Eubanks Davis, founder of Braven; Nancy Sanchez, chief opportunity office of Phi Theta Kappa Honor Society; and Steve Bumbaugh, senior vice president for college, career, and digital access at the College Board—about the risky message college critics are sending. Yes, any policy reformer can make good-faith arguments in favor of the need for better degree alternatives. But Eubanks Davis, Sanchez, and Bumbaugh all say this kind of advice often amounts to recommending something for other people's children—disproportionately Black and Latino children—that the advice givers wouldn't encourage their own kids to do.

In brief, building one's own human capital through education is like investing in a lasting asset. True, earning a bachelor's degree is no guarantee of career success. But the odds are generally good. As discussed in the second chapter of this book, extensive evidence shows the economic benefits that typically accrue to people with degrees (along with many others, from good health to civic involvement, that are not the focus of this volume). A BA "ends up being the gold standard, because that's what employers hire," economist Anthony Carnevale, director of the Georgetown University Center on Education and the Workforce, told me.[2] "I think there is intelligence in markets. And given the millions and millions of decisions that are made by employers about who to hire and who to promote, it suggests to me that they find that [degrees] work." For the many people who could benefit, raising college attendance and completion rates simply makes sense.

The Second Career Art:
Find the Best *Kind* of College and Program

It's also important to note that college is not a one-size-fits-all experience. Anybody considering college does not have to make a stark choice between an arcane academic experience and practical vocational preparation. This notion continues to dog discussions about broadening postsecondary educational access. Yet it remains a false dichotomy.

We can reasonably stipulate that a greater number of purposeful career-oriented options would be helpful and attractive to many students. What skeptics of the access agenda often miss, when they declare knowingly that not everyone is cut out for college, is just how much vocational education already exists within the very large umbrella of our postsecondary system. The question is what exactly we mean by the word college. The world of two- and four-year degrees includes a multitude of options.

An undergraduate interested in exploring the life of the mind, or immersing herself in a traditional, rigorous academic field, can opt to major in a field like philosophy or theoretical physics. Depending on the general education requirements of the college they attend, graduates with those majors are also likely to have written papers, studied history or social science, analyzed data, and perhaps studied a foreign language. Many will acquire a useful mixture of broad education and specific expertise. They might go on to a job, to a master's or PhD program leading to an academic or research career, or to a professional school in fields like law, medicine, or engineering. But many other bachelor's degree students graduate with majors that have immediate, practical career value: nursing (about 13 percent of all undergraduate degrees are in health professions),[3] computer science (about 5 percent),[4] teaching (about 4 percent),[5] engineering (about 7 percent),[6] and more. The single most popular college major is business (making up about one in five bachelor's degrees when subfields like marketing, finance, and accounting are included),[7] which is hardly an abstruse, theoretical subject.

For a large number of students—around 33 percent of the national total—undergraduate education means community college.[8] Again, this extremely popular set of institutions doesn't provide anything close to a uniform experience, and certainly nothing approaching the ivory tower stereotype of college. Some students attend to take advantage of low-cost classes that provide the general education requirements they will need to transfer and graduate from a four-year institution (although many more should be succeeding at this goal). Others are focused on career-focused associate degrees in a range of career-oriented specialties.

Many who opt for community college aren't seeking a cloistered undergraduate campus but welcome a college experience that can be integrated fairly smoothly with jobs, family obligations, and other important aspects of their lives. This, too, is college. And despite challenges, community colleges remain extremely well positioned to offer large numbers of students an educational opportunity squarely at the intersection of broad academic skills, professional training, and workforce needs.

For the expanding number of middle-skill jobs in fields that are being quickly transformed by technological innovation, employers are seeking precisely what community colleges can deliver. According to interviews with more than two hundred administrators, faculty, and staff at eight community colleges, employers are increasingly stressing four sets of skills in the key occupational categories of allied health, information technology, and advanced manufacturing. Foundational skills in math, reading, and writing fall in the first. Technical skills required for specific jobs fall in the second. The third consists of digital literacy skills. The fourth category, according to a 2022 report on the study by the Community College Research Center and MIT's Task Force on the Work of the Future, requires "a broad mix of interpersonal and cognitive skills central to collaboration, critical thinking, and customer service."[9] To be sure, a full associate degree may not be required in every case. But the researchers recommend better alignment between short-term certificate programs and longer-term degree programs, as discussed below.

The Third Career Art:
Complete College

For anyone who decides to pursue an undergraduate education, whether at a two-year or four-year institution, it's important to do as much as possible to finish. Degree completion remains valuable currency in the labor market and a prerequisite for numerous advanced credentials. The extensive positive data on economic outcomes cited in this volume are for college graduates, who unfortunately make up too small a percentage of those who begin their undergraduate studies. Disappointing national completion rates help account for the enormous number of Americans—thirty-nine million at last count—who report their highest level of education as "some college, no degree." Community colleges, who serve a different mixture of students than do four-year institutions, report even more dismal associate degree completion rates, particularly given the high percentages of students who report that they begin at community college with the intent of transferring to bachelor's-granting institutions.

What about the economic benefits of earning some college credits, even without obtaining a degree? Research here is mixed, but a large study of Texas high school graduates found relatively higher rates of employment and higher earnings for those who had some college compared to their peers with only high school diplomas.[10] This suggests that the argument against encouraging more students to try college, even at the risk of noncompletion, is often misguided in purely financial terms. Still, even with variations by subject studied, average earnings for degree holders are so much higher than for noncompleters that graduation should remain a high priority.

Although it's understandable that rising college costs, along with rising student debt (as well as loans taken out by parents) has alarmed many Americans, it remains the case that low-income students in particular often overestimate the cost of college and underestimate the amount of financial aid that's available. Some undergraduates trying to make ends meet work long hours at part-time jobs in order to avoid borrowing. But excessive work hours can lead students not to complete their degrees. Conversely, borrowing at a reasonable level in order to make timely progress to graduation makes as much if not more sense than other common borrowing behavior—for a house or a car, for instance. The principle of providing loans to people who lack both education and financial resources in order for them to develop their human capital and improve their value in the labor market is perfectly defensible. Taking on debt without earning the degree that makes repayment more likely to be manageable puts this trade-off in jeopardy.

Just as students should make a priority of making it to graduation, colleges and universities themselves have a significant role to play in improving their prospects of success. Fortunately, the days are long past when college lore had deans telling incoming freshmen: "Look to your left. Look to your right. Only one of you will graduate."[11] Weeding out struggling students is no longer regarded as something to brag about or as an indicator of a degree program's rigor but is now seen as a problem to be solved. Growing recognition that academic deficits are by no means the biggest barrier to persistence for many undergraduates has led many campuses to focus on wraparound supports that range from personalized advising, to emergency loans or food assistance, to academic and financial assistance.

Data analytics play a growing role on many campuses as a sort of advance-warning system that flags students and professors about the need to check in more regularly about assignments and exams. Tutoring may help, as might broader coaching of the kind provided by nonprofits like Inside Track that work in partnership with colleges. A major analysis of twenty years of randomized control trials by the social policy research organization MDRC found that two approaches were most likely to help community college students make academic progress: a multifaceted set of supports to address multiple barriers faced by students, and promoting full-time en-rollment.[12] The research also found promising results from students' use of advising and academic tutoring, and to some extent financial assistance.

The Fourth Career Art:
If Pursuing Nondegree Options, Purposefully
Build Education, Skills, and Networks

Before the disruption brought by the Covid-19 pandemic, close to seven in ten recent American high school graduates were enrolled in a two- or four-year college. That still leaves millions with no college plans, whether they intend to go straight to work, enter the military, or, in relatively small numbers, begin an apprenticeship. Many more students start college and for a variety of reasons, from fit to finances, don't continue. College may not be right for everybody. Yet it's important for everyone hoping to improve their career prospects to understand just how much economic changes over time have made some kind of education and training after high school more important than ever for economic advancement.

The good news is that large public demand for affordable, short-term, nondegree credentials and training has led to a huge number of these offerings—more than one million. To be sure, this frequently cited count from the nonprofit Credential Engine is based on an expansive definition; it uses every possible variation on each kind of secondary and postsecondary degree, license, certificate, digital badge, and more. Still, even the sixteen core categories in this census of credentials yield a potentially confusing range of options. And making

informed choices based on the quality and return on investment of these options requires close scrutiny of much more
than the costs and time required for a program or credential.
Proven models like Year Up, discussed in chapter 3, and Per
Scholas are fairly short and are carefully constructed to provide participants with a mixture of broad professional soft
skills and targeted skills connected to job market needs. They
include practical, hands-on work experience and access to
new networks. They can be completed concurrently with
community college classes, or for those who want to start on
a career immediately, they certainly leave the door open for
more study at some point in the future.

Seeking career-focused education that leads to occupations with good starting wages and attractive benefits is an
important starting point. Research points to the value of occupational training in high-growth sectors like health care,
information technology, and manufacturing. Finding pathways that have opportunities for advancement is also a key
consideration. Harvard Business School professor Joseph
Fuller, coleader of the HBS Managing the Future of Work
initiative, offers the example of two programs at Boston's
Bunker Hill Community College, one leading to pharmacy
tech certification and the other preparing graduates for IT
help desk jobs. Each requires the same number of credit
hours, he explained in an interview. But the pharmacy tech
field doesn't pay very well and, worse, is "a complete island"
with no promising career path. By contrast, IT help desk jobs
pay 60 percent more on average and provide the prior experience needed as a building block for multiple other positions
in the IT sector.

Despite all the attention paid in public discussion to non-degree credentials as an alternative to college, in fact the majority of people seeking to build specific skills through tailored education programs actually possess degrees already. At the same time, interest in alternative credentials, fueled partly by rising college costs, has grown among people who either have never attended college or didn't complete their degree. In either case, whether a recent high school graduate wants to gain job skills in the short term, or a middle-aged college graduate plans to change fields with newly acquired knowledge, identifying programs in fields with strong labor market demand is a good place to start.

Organizations like Emsi Burning Glass, which was rebranded in 2022 as Lightcast, have shown in concrete detail how different jobs require varying combinations of discrete skills. This applies even within the same occupational sector. A computer programmer in one region of the country may require a different mixture of programming languages and other abilities than does a programmer in a different region, or even within the same state.[13] This means that choosing a nondegree credential requires a clear understanding of the skills an individual already possesses, the mixture needed for in-demand jobs, and which specific skills can be added to make that person an attractive candidate for hiring.

As discussed in chapter 3, certain job categories that don't pay very well (and are disproportionately held by Black and Latino workers) may combine several skills that, with one or two additions, would make those employees competitive for better-paid positions in related jobs that require a fairly similar set of skills. Understanding these specific job market needs, with assistance navigating the decision-making process, should position those individuals to make smart decisions about which nondegree credentials will help them get ahead professionally.

To separate the wheat from the chaff among short-term credentials, asking questions about where a credential leads beyond the first job is vital. It's not enough to be certain that acquiring an in-demand skill with a recognized credential will help an individual get hired. The first job should have the potential to lead to other positions in the same sector, so the credential is the first building block toward upward mobility.

Seeking stackable credentials that lead to credit and ultimately degrees is also an especially promising approach to picking nondegree education options, especially for people who either didn't start college or never finished. Earning a short-term credential, which may be useful for earning a raise or a promotion, or switching to a new job or even a new field, has even greater appeal when it bears academic credit. That allows the student to continue working and earning money, and then return to class when time permits to add more skills, additional credentials, and eventually a full two- or four-year degree, with the long-term value typically associated with college diplomas.

This increasingly popular approach allows learners to seek the best of both worlds: they can acquire targeted skills quickly, at modest cost, while incrementally making progress toward full degrees. One proponent is Anant Agarwal, a long-time MIT professor and the founder of the pioneering MOOC (Massive Open Online Course) provider edX. He told me in a *Higher Ed Spotlight* podcast interview that edX offers a micro master's credential in soft skills like critical thinking and communication—a helpful acknowledgment that technical skills and broader skills should go hand in hand. Stacking credentials is far better than the longtime practice of those who complete only part of a degree program having nothing to show for it, he says. "If somewhere along the way you decide you've had enough of learning after one year, and you leave, they call you a dropout."[14]

The Fifth Career Art:
Seek a Both/And Combination of Broad and Targeted Skills

Long-term career success requires a mixture of broad capabilities and targeted skills. So whether an individual is pursuing a college degree or an alternative such as a skills-based credential, it's best not to think of these options as completely separate pathways. As University of Virginia economist Sarah Turner points out, "that's a false distinction" because vocational education and core academics aren't completely separate. "There are basic science components and basic humanities components in many of the career and technical programs," she says. "You need to learn some science to become a certified auto mechanic— you need to know something about Pascal's law, which has to do with hydraulics. And by the way, it's not as if all my undergraduates know Pascal's law."[15]

In brief, the choice is not an either/or decision. To equip people with the best mixture of education and skills they need to find a both/and strategy for acquiring what they need.

Degrees come in many shapes and sizes, with varying returns, but generally speaking anyone pursuing that route may be in luck simply because the package of a subject-specific major and a series of more general classes should help graduates develop necessary analytical and communications skills along with more targeted skills. At the same time, it remains important for students and the institutions that serve them to be purposeful about ensuring that both broad and focused skills developed in college studies are connected to careers.

The fundamental aims of postsecondary education certainly include pursuit of knowledge for its own sake. Yet it is no longer particularly controversial to note that many students go to college to prepare for careers. Recognizing this common goal is by no means a betrayal of the university's mission, particularly given how straightforward it is to make the case that nonvocational majors in the liberal arts are in fact extremely helpful preparation for long-term career success.

This isn't just a job for the campus career office. Academic leaders can do a lot to build awareness of how particular experiences and skills, from working in teams to clearly synthesizing research findings, are useful in the workforce. Professors also have vital career guidance to offer as trusted sources of information and connections. Faculty are sometimes wary of being thrust into the role of job coaches, but what students value is something quite different: explanations of how their classroom studies are connected to career possibilities and the range of specific and broad skills employers value.

This can happen even at institutions well known for their commitment to liberal arts. At highly selective Wellesley College, for example, neuroscience professor Sara Wasserman runs a capstone seminar in which she regularly invites professionals in the field to speak to undergraduates about a range of careers. Across the country in San Diego, California, Point Loma Nazarene University has created a "major map" for each academic major. Developed by academic program leaders together with career services staff, each major map shows which career-readiness skills students develop in the academic specialty. It also shows the range of career paths alumni of the small, faith-based liberal arts university have taken.[16] Similarly, Kenyon College shows prospective students and their parents "the actual job trajectories of graduates from each of its majors in what looks like the route map at the back of an airline magazine," as described by the *Hechinger Report*.[17] "We give them concrete information that addresses the concern or anxiety that my son or daughter will major in English and not be employable on the other side," says Sean Decatur, president of the Ohio liberal arts college. "We need to get more comfortable in talking about the fact that our students do get jobs, that we actually *want* them to get jobs."[18]

Even more than being taught about how education and careers are connected, students have much to gain by trying out different professional experiences themselves as undergraduates. Career-relevant part-time and summer jobs, along with internships, are extremely useful for this reason. The value of gaining experience, learning firsthand about translating classroom skills to the workforce, proving one's abilities, and building professional relationships is hard to overstate. That these experiences are much less common for low-income and first-generation college students is one reason for the push to eliminate unpaid internships, improve financial aid, and seek other ways to level the playing field when it comes to integrating education and skills.

The need to apply broad and targeted skills, both by gaining professional experience and by approaching educational decisions purposefully, works in both directions, of course. Anybody who chooses not to pursue a degree in the near term should keep in mind that the appeal and usefulness of developing immediate job skills needs to be balanced with acquiring broader skills in areas like communication, teamwork, analyzing big-picture trends, and contributing to long-term projects. A huge proportion of jobs in growing sectors require broad, soft skills as well as specific vocational talents. Even in STEM careers that might appear to be highly technical, career progress into management roles is likely to rely on a broad range of abilities, as research by David Deming, Brent Orrell, and others has shown.

What's more, my former Strada Education Network colleague Michelle Weise notes in her 2020 book *Long Life Learning* that significantly longer life spans will be accompanied by the need to navigate many more job and career changes.[19] This development has implications not only for the need to reskill and upskill as the specific needs of the labor market shift. It will also require the general capacities that are called for to navigate multiple workforce transitions.

The Sixth Career Art:
Take Advantage of Employer-Funded Education Benefits

Building general and targeted skills by taking college classes or other kinds of education and training does not require dropping everything else going on in a person's life, including paid work. Nor does it require having large sums of money saved up for education or taking on student debt. A growing number of employers, including corporate giants like Walmart, Amazon, Starbucks, and McDonald's, have introduced or expanded employee education benefits that allow workers to learn and earn at the same time.

Historically, corporate education benefits have been underused. A big obstacle was the policy of many employers to reimburse tuition costs only after classes were completed; being required to pay tuition out-of-pocket served as a disincentive for many workers to participate. Now many firms pay employees' tuition up front, which has boosted participation rates—Chipotle introduced its debt-free degree program in 2019 and saw a "significant increase" in employee participation.[20]

Balancing work and study is not always easy, but acquiring new skills is extremely helpful to make progress within a job or switch to another. Amazon, which has significantly expanded its education benefits through its giant Career Choice program, works with nearby education providers to offer classes that are closely connected to open jobs in the local community that pay at least 10 percent more than Amazon's wages. "It needs to be a job that has a career path," says Ardine Williams, who oversaw the initiative as Amazon's vice president for education.[21] "Not a cul-de-sac job, like a pharmacy tech, where once you get certification you're sort of stuck. The credits earned should serve as the scaffolding to that next career level, certification, and pay rise." The company helps hourly workers change their schedules to allow them to attend classes, which are often offered in on-site classrooms with outside instructors. At a time when more Americans are seeking work that helps them build their human capital, offering education benefits to open up new career paths is "the new minimum wage," Williams says.

The Seventh Career Art:
Find Effective Ways to Build Social Capital

A broad education and targeted skills are two vital components of career success. But neither will be effective without the third leg of the stool: social capital. Personal relationships, connections, and introductions play an instrumental role in how individuals learn about which employers are hiring and which jobs are open. The same networks help people get recommended, get hired, and gain experience. Then the skills and working relationships they develop in turn allow them to progress through the labor force.

Everybody needs help developing these relationships and networks. Many young people from middle-class and affluent backgrounds acquire them from families, schools, and communities filled with people who have graduated from college and navigated the professional world with considerable success. Those with fewer inherited advantages also have families and networks. But they often require more guidance about how to gather information about jobs, how to make a persuasive case for themselves, and how to develop the professional ties that will help them get ahead. Like Brooklyn College graduate Farzana Chowdhury, whose story is recounted in chapter 4, they are likely to find that earning a degree is necessary for labor market success, but not sufficient.

Building social capital can take place in many settings, both formal and informal. Beyond the network building that should take place on college campuses or in alternative credential programs, but too often does not, a number of programs explicitly aim to tap latent social capital. Some, including Braven and COOP Careers, are designed for degree holders. Other nonprofits like Climb Hire focus on individuals who may not have degrees and seek to move beyond the gig economy into jobs with more promising career ladders. Groups such as Social Capital Builders offer a range of classes and training sessions for teens through partners like Catholic Charities and regional workforce organizations. And of course platforms like LinkedIn and Handshake offer users the chance to take the initiative to connect with existing and potential professional contacts.

The value of direct advice on the practical steps needed to build networks can't be underestimated. Braven founder Aimée Eubanks Davis published a useful set of tips in *Ascend—Harvard Business Review* for how first-generation students can build networks, with a focus on LinkedIn.[22] She covers everything from how to write a headline to how to build connections to what to ask during networking conversations to sustain relationships. Credentials and intellect aren't all it takes to get ahead, and access to connections may be unequal. But, she writes, in words that apply to much more than just social capital, "if you focus on what is in your control, you don't have to wait for the world to change."

Educators, counselors, and others who work directly with young people also need guidance on the best ways to help high school and postsecondary students build and strengthen their networks, and thus widen their career prospects. A playbook created by the Christensen Institute outlines five steps for building and strengthening students' networks, from evaluating their social capital to expanding their networks to leveraging educational technology. It gives the example of Beyond 12, the nonprofit described in chapter 4 that offers virtual coaching to historically underrepresented, low-income, first-generation college students. Beyond 12 coaches use a checklist to measure specific steps students can take to build their on-campus networks. One item is to identify a campus advocate or mentor. Another is to identify three peers who can serve as references. The third is to create at least one study group with high-performing peers.[23]

Beyond these concrete measures, many proponents of building social capital urge individual students and those who advise them to take an asset-based rather than a deficit-based approach to developing networks. The point is to build on the strengths and existing social capital people possess rather than assuming that something in their background is broken and needs to be fixed. It may be a semantic distinction, but the practical advice is useful because it tells students that they can adapt their existing social skills and familiar customs to be successful in what might otherwise be an intimidating professional networking process. That's what Beyond 12 coaches do when they ask students to map their own networks—both the people who have helped them get where they are and those they have supported. Beyond 12's chief knowledge officer, Eve Shapiro, describes this practice as a "way in" for coaches to connect the network building and advice seeking that students have already done off campus to the similar efforts they need to make in college.[24]

In a similar vein, college career services veteran Christine Cruzvergara, chief education strategy officer at Handshake, routinely advises students that the same approach they take to making friends when they arrive on campus can be used to develop the relationships they need to create professional networks. "That process of building relationships is not any different than what you would do when you need to network. And in fact the peers that you are meeting are part of your network," she told me in a podcast interview. "But many students don't think of it that way . . . as a skill that they're going to use later when they are trying to meet an alum or professional or go to a formal networking event. . . . We just have to draw the connection for them."[25]

Nolvia Delgado, who immigrated to the United States from the Dominican Republic at age five and went on to transfer from the Borough of Manhattan Community College to Smith College,[26] gives comparable advice. Now executive director of the Kaplan Educational Foundation, she likes to remind students that familiar cultural traditions like gathering for a *cafecito*, coffee and conversation, or seeking *consejo*, advice about big decisions or dilemmas from family and community elders, can be adapted to the relationship building and advice seeking that is central to professional networking.

The Eighth Career Art: Prepare for the World as It Is, Not as You Wish It Were

A couple of months into my book research, I walked along the Charles River near Harvard's Kennedy School with David Deming, the policy school's academic dean and the Isabelle and Scott Black Professor of Political Economy. One of the first things he told me was that before thinking about which credentials to recommend, it's important to evaluate the labor market's need for different kinds of skills. He contrasted the broad skills college provides with tailored, short-term skills programs that operate more like "finishing schools."[27]

Each has its place. Deming is sympathetic to the need to provide more pathways for people who want to learn practical skills without going through a full degree program. But targeted skills become obsolete. Broad skills acquired in degree programs can be useful throughout an individual's career and can be supplemented as needed with market-ready education and training. That's why Deming would like to improve the access and affordability of publicly funded higher education and thus create a bigger pool of people with the most flexible educational background for lifelong career progress.

The framework Deming outlines should be kept in mind by anybody who is trying to make sense of claims that degrees aren't worthwhile and that growing numbers of jobs don't require these out-of-favor qualifications.

True, there's no mistaking strong public interest in expanding affordable short-term options for education and training beyond degrees. For many people, growing calls for more hiring and promotions based on skills rather than formal degree qualifications hold intuitive appeal. Anybody who navigated the enormous disruptions of the Covid-19 pandemic knows how quickly the labor market, and everything else, can change. So it makes sense for anybody seeking to advance professionally to pay careful attention to changes in formal credential requirements and, more importantly, actual hiring behavior.

In some cases, as organizations like Opportunity@Work advocate and states like Maryland have implemented, it will be possible to show how an individual's skills and experience qualify them for open jobs, without the overlay of excessive credentialism.

Yet students and those who work with them need to know about present-day realities along with emerging and future trends. For most people it still makes sense to be prepared for the world as it is, not the world others are hoping for. It would be a terrible mistake if we pretended degrees weren't a huge advantage in getting ahead, and overlooked the educational decisions so many people with advantages make for themselves and their own children. Yes, degree requirements can be a barrier, but so is a failure to build human capital. Equipping more Americans with degrees, including more from low-income backgrounds, more African Americans, and more Latinos, will help those individuals and help the nation.

The Georgetown University Center on Education and the Workforce concisely reminds us of the available evidence about the payoff to getting more education rather than less. Median earnings go up with each level of education. Earning a certificate boosts earnings by 20 percent on average compared to an individual with just a high school diploma. An associate degree increases the earning premium to 32 percent. Those with a bachelor's degree make 74 percent more on average than workers with a high school diploma. Earning a graduate degree more than doubles the median earnings increase.[28] Indeed, while considerable public attention has been focused on master's degree programs with poor return on investment that leave graduates in heavy debt, there's good reason for continued robust enrollment in many graduate programs: the same charts that illustrate the large and continuing wage premium for bachelor's degree holders show even greater economic returns for individuals with graduate degrees.

Degrees alone are not the be all and end all, of course. As Deming's comments on skills indicate, some version of reskilling and upskilling over time is likely to be needed for degree holders and non–college graduates alike. In a both/and world, the comparison offered by Futuro Health CEO Van Ton-Quinlivan, former executive vice chancellor of the California Community Colleges, of education as a periodic booster shot, rather than an up-front inoculation for life,[29] will serve many people well.

Conclusion

This book has offered a rebuttal to the false dichotomy between college and practical skills that mars the public and policy debate over postsecondary education. At a time when long-term economic changes increasingly require education beyond high school for career success, too many Americans doubt the proven value of college. They also receive too little guidance about the best alternatives or supplements that will provide them, over time, with the optimal combination of broad and targeted skills needed to keep them productively employed in a fast-changing labor market. Even when a range of pathways to acquire these skills is available, disadvantaged Americans often don't get help building the networks and tools they need to navigate the route to sustainable success.

It's time for us to do better. The United States, and the many other countries facing similar demands for more and better education in a changing labor market, can do more to adopt a both/and approach to improving people's career prospects and to fostering upward mobility. Policy makers, educators, employers, students, and engaged citizens need to understand, replicate, and pursue the best models for success in both traditional and nontraditional educational pathways. They should also embrace the need for greater attention to social capital. We can build on our many successes, and also learn from our shortcomings, as we forge a fresh approach to expanding broad and targeted educational opportunities for more Americans in order to improve their chances of lifelong career success.

Notes

Chapter 1

1. US Census Bureau, "CPS Historical Time Series Visualizations," February 24, 2022, https://www.census.gov/library/visualizations/time-series/demo/cps-historical-time-series.html.

2. "Family Voices: Building Pathways from Learning to Meaningful Work," Carnegie Corporation of New York and Gallup, April 7, 2021, https://media.carnegie.org/filer_public/65/88/6588ffd2-561a-4c98-a8fd-b39730ddd100/carnegie_gallup_family_voices_final_report_040221.pdf.

3. Josh Moody, "A 5th Straight Semester of Enrollment Declines," *Inside Higher Ed*, May 26, 2022, https://www.insidehighered.com/news/2022/05/26/nsc-report-shows-total-enrollment-down-41-percent.

4. Carrie Besnette Hauser and Jamie Merisotis, "The Promise of Dual-Mission Colleges," *Inside Higher Ed*, February 4, 2021, https://www.insidehighered.com/views/2021/02/04/dual-mission-colleges-offer-novel-and-needed-approach-higher-education-opinion.

5. Author interview with Carrie Besnette Hauser, video, April 7, 2022; and Carrie Besnette Hauser, personal communication with author, August 26, 2022.

6. Matthew Sigelman, Scott Bittle, Will Markow, and Benjamin Francis, "The Hybrid Job Economy: How New Skills Are Rewriting the DNA of the Job Market," Burning Glass, January 20, 2019, https://www.economicmodeling.com/wp-content/uploads/2022/05/hybrid_jobs_2019_final.pdf.

7. Lauren Weber, "The 'Hybrid' Skills That Tomorrow's Jobs Will Require," *Wall Street Journal*, January 22, 2019, https://www.wsj.com/articles/the-hybrid-skills-that-tomorrows-jobs-will-require-11547994266.

8. Author interview with Matt Sigelman, Washington, DC, December 14, 2021.

9. David J. Deming, "The Value of Soft Skills in the Labor Market," *NBER Reporter*, December 2017, https://www.nber.org/reporter/2017number4/value-soft-skills-labor-market.

10. David Deming, "In the Salary Race, Engineers Sprint but English Majors Endure," *New York Times*, September 20, 2019, https://www.nytimes.com/2019/09/20/business/liberal-arts-stem-salaries.html.

11. Jill Barshay, "Proof Points: The Number of College Graduates in the Humanities Drops for the Eighth Consecutive Year," *Hechinger Report*, November 22, 2021, https://hechingerreport.org/proof-points-the-number-of-college-graduates-in-the-humanities-drops-for-the-eighth-consecutive-year/.

12. Deming, "In the Salary Race."

13. Ibid.

14. Brent Orrell, ed., *Minding Our Workforce: The Role of Noncognitive Skills in Career Success* (Washington, DC: American Enterprise Institute, 2021), 5, https://www.aei.org/wp-content/uploads/2021/05/Minding-our-Workforce.pdf?x91208.

15. Ben Wildavsky and Aimée Eubanks Davis, "David Deming," *Lessons Earned* podcast, Strada Education Network, February 24, 2021, https://stradaeducation.org/podcast/david-deming/.

16. Paul Fain, "Alternative Credentials on the Rise," *Inside Higher Ed*, August 27, 2020, https://www.insidehighered.com/news/2020/08/27/interest-spikes-short-term-online-credentials-will-it-be-sustained.

17. Ibid.

18. Kenneth Adams et al., "Community College Presidents Letter," September 8, 2021, https://opportunityamericaonline.org/wp-content/uploads/2021/09/community-college-presidents-letter.pdf.

19. Author interview with Joseph Fuller, Cambridge, MA, October 4, 2021.

20. "The Paper Ceiling," Opportunity@Work, announced June 2022, https://opportunityatwork.org/thepaperceiling/?utm_campaign=The%20Job&utm_medium=email&utm_source=Revue%20newsletter, accessed February 6, 2023.

21. Joseph B. Fuller, Christina Langer, Julia Nitschke, Layla O'Kane, Matt Sigelman, and Bledi Taska, "The Emerging Degree Reset," Burning Glass Institute, 2022, https://www.burningglassinstitute.org/research/the-emerging-degree-reset.

22. Lindsay Daugherty, "A College Degree Is No Longer Always the Best Pathway to the Middle Class: That Might Me a Good Thing," *Fortune*, April 5, 2022, https://fortune.com/2022/04/05/college-degree-tuition-costs-certificates-apprenticeship/.

23. Rebecca Koenig, "Employers Claim to Value Alternative Credentials: Do Their Practices Match Their Promises?," EdSurge, April 20, 2022, https://www.edsurge.com/news/2022-04-20-employers-claim-to-value-alternative-credentials-do-their-practices-match-their-promises?utm_content=206137778&utm_medium=social&utm_source=linkedin&hss_channel=lcp-1043639.

24. Fuller et al., "Emerging Degree Reset."

25. Author interview with Matt Sigelman, telephone, February 8, 2022.

26. Scott Bittle, personal email communication, February 9, 2022.

27. Christina Langer, personal email communication, November 17, 2022.

28. Gad Levanon, LinkedIn post, December 2022, https://www.linkedin.com/posts/gad-levanon-3b9b933_hiring-education-collegedegree-activity-7010971318510604289-y65Z/?utm_source=share&utm_medium=member_ios, accessed February 10, 2023.

29. Courtney Connley, "Google, Apple and 12 Other Companies That No Longer Require Employees to Have a College Degree," CNBC, October 8, 2018, https://www.cnbc.com/2018/08/16/15-companies-that-no-longer-require-employees-to-have-a-college-degree.html.

30. Author interview with Sean Gallagher, Boston, October 5, 2021.

31. Author interview with Maggie Johnson, video, June 27, 2022.

32. Maggie Johnson, personal email communication, June 28, 2022.

33. Jaison R. Abel and Richard Deitz, "Despite Rising Costs, College Is Still a Good Investment," Federal Reserve Bank of New York, June 5, 2019, https://libertystreeteconomics.newyorkfed.org/2019/06/despite-rising-costs-college-is-still-a-good-investment/.

34. Chauncy Lennon, "College or Short-Term Credential? First, Check Your Assumptions," Work Shift, September 15, 2021, https://workshift.opencampusmedia.org/college-or-short-term-credential-first-check-your-assumptions/.

35. Matthew Sigelman, "Getting Past the Lazy Debate," Inside Higher Ed, February 8, 2016, https://www.insidehighered.com/views/2016/02/08/debate-over-liberal-arts-vs-vocationalism-lazy-one-essay.

36. For more on the "false choice" between liberal arts and applied education, see "The Future of Undergraduate Education: The Future of America," Commission on the Future of Undergraduate Education, American Academy of Arts and Sciences, 2017, https://www.amacad.org/sites/default/files/publication/downloads/Future-of-Undergraduate-Education.pdf. See also Michelle R. Weise, Andrew R. Hanson, Rob Sentz, Yustina Saleh, "Robot-Ready: Human+ Skills for the Future of Work," Strada Institute for the Future of Work, Emsi, November 1,

2018, https://apo.org.au/sites/default/files/resource-files/2018-11/apo-nid209116 .pdf.

37. Andrew Hanson "Examining the Value of Nondegree Credentials," Strada Center for Education Consumer Insights, July 28, 2021, https://cci.stradaeducation .org/pv-release-july-28-2021/#.

38. Author interview with Meghan Hughes, video, December 1, 2021.

39. Claudia Goldin and Lawrence F. Katz, *The Race between Education and Technology* (Cambridge, MA: Harvard University Press, 2008).

40. Edward DeJesus, "Social Capital for Youth Economic Mobility," webinar, Institute for Social Capital, April 1, 2022, https://www.socialcapitalresearch.com /event/webinar-edward-dejesus/.

41. John Clark, "College Alumni See Room for Job-Skill Improvement" Gallup, July 14, 2020, https://news.gallup.com/poll/315500/college-alumni-room-job -skill-improvement.aspx.

42. Author interview with Kalani Leifer, San Francisco, November 11, 2021.

43. Lucinda Gray, Laurie Lewis, and John Ralph, "Career and Technical Education Programs in Public School Districts: 2016–17," National Center for Education Statistics, April 2018, https://nces.ed.gov/pubs2018/2018028.pdf.

Chapter 2

1. Author interview with Susan Dynarski, Cambridge, MA, October 3, 2021.

2. Ibid.

3. Susan Dynarski, "ACT/SAT for All: A Cheap, Effective Way to Narrow Income Gaps in College," Brookings, February 8, 2018, https://www.brookings.edu/research /act-sat-for-all-a-cheap-effective-way-to-narrow-income-gaps-in-college/.

4. Susan Dynarski, "Fafsa Follies: To Gain a Student, Eliminate a Form," *New York Times*, August 21, 2015, https://www.nytimes.com/2015/08/23/upshot/fafsa -follies-to-gain-a-student-eliminate-a-form.html?.

5. Claudia Goldin and Lawrence F. Katz, *The Race between Education and Technology* (Cambridge, MA: Harvard University Press, 2008).

6. "Research Summary: Education and Lifetime Earnings," Social Security Administration, https://www.ssa.gov/policy/docs/research-summaries/education -earnings.html. This report also states that median lifetime earnings are $655,000 more for men with bachelor's degrees and $450,000 more for women with bachelor's degree than for their high school graduate counterparts, after controlling for socioeconomic factors that influence salaries and likelihood of college completion.

7. "The Labor Market for Recent College Graduates," Federal Reserve Bank of New York, February 12, 2021, https://www.newyorkfed.org/research/college-labor-market/college-labor-market_wages.html.

8. Seth D. Zimmerman, "The Returns to College Admission for Academically Marginal Students," *Journal of Labor Economics* 32, no. 4 (2014): 711–54, https://doi.org/10.1086/676661.

9. Ben Ost, Weixiang Pan, and Douglas Webber, "The Returns to College Persistence for Marginal Students: Regression Discontinuity Evidence from University Dismissal Policies," *Journal of Labor Economics* 36, no. 3 (2018): 779–805, https://doi.org/10.1086/696204.

10. See, for example, Anthony C. Carnevale, Ban Cheah, and Andrew R. Hanson, "The Economic Value of College Majors," Georgetown University Center on Education and the Workforce, May 7, 2015, https://cewgeorgetown.wpenginepowered.com/wp-content/uploads/The-Economic-Value-of-College-Majors-Full-Report-web-FINAL.pdf.

11. Susan H. Greenberg, "Judging a Degree by the Program, Not the College," *Inside Higher Ed*, September 16, 2021, https://www.insidehighered.com/news/2021/09/16/studies-pick-college-programs-best-investment-returns.

12. David Deming, "In the Salary Race, Engineers Sprint but English Majors Endure," *New York Times*, September 20, 2019, https://www.nytimes.com/2019/09/20/business/liberal-arts-stem-salaries.html.

13. Author interview with Anthony Carnevale, video, August 27, 2021.

14. Author interview with Josh Wyner, video, November 4, 2021.

15. Anthony P. Carnevale, Tanya I. Garcia, Neil Ridley, and Michael C. Quinn, "The Overlooked Value of Certificates and Associate's Degrees," Georgetown University Center on Education and the Workforce, January 28, 2020, https://cewgeorgetown.wpenginepowered.com/wp-content/uploads/CEW-SubBA.pdfpdf.

16. Ibid.

17. John Bound, Michael F. Lovenheim, and Sarah Turner, "Why Have College Completion Rates Declined? An Analysis of Changing Student Preparation and Collegiate Resources," *American Economic Journal: Applied Economics* 2, no. 3 (2010), https://www.aeaweb.org/articles?id=10.1257/app.2.3.129.

18. Jeffrey T. Denning, Eric R. Eide, and Merrill Warnick, "Why Have College Completion Rates Increased?," *American Economic Journal: Applied Economics* 14, no. 3 (2022), https://www.aeaweb.org/articles?id=10.1257/app.20200525.

19. Victoria Yuen, "New Insights into Attainment for Low-Income Students," Center for American Progress, February 21, 2019, https://www.americanprogress.org/article/new-insights-attainment-low-income-students/.

20. "Community College Transfer," Aspen Institute, https://highered.aspeninstitute.org/community-college-transfer/, accessed February 7, 2023.

21. Carnevale et al., "Overlooked Value of Certificates and Associate's Degrees."

22. Jennifer Causey, Hee Sun Kim, Mikyung Ryu, Abigail Scheetz, and Doug Shapiro, "Some College, No Credential Student Outcomes, Annual Progress Report—Academic Year 2020/21," National Student Clearinghouse Research Center, May 2022, https://nscresearchcenter.org/wp-content/uploads/SCNCReportMay2022.pdf.

23. Elyse Ashburn, "Community College Students Are Disappearing," *Work Shift*, October 26, 2021, https://workshift.opencampusmedia.org/community-college-students-are-disappearing/?utm_campaign=The%20Job&utm_medium=email&utm_source=Revue%20newsletter.

24. "Total Fall Enrollment in Degree-Granting Postsecondary Institutions, by Control and Level of Institution: 1970 through 2019," National Center for Education Statistics, January 2021, https://nces.ed.gov/programs/digest/d20/tables/dt20_303.25.asp?utm_campaign=The%20Job&utm_medium=email&utm_source=Revue%20newsletter.

25. Ashburn, "Community College Students Are Disappearing."

26. Greg Johnson, "W.Va. Chef Richard Rosendale Is Out to Win the Bocuse d'Or Cooking Competition," *Washington Post*, December 13, 2012, https://www.washingtonpost.com/lifestyle/magazine/wva-chef-richard-rosendale-is-out-to-win-the-bocuse-dor-cooking-competition/2012/12/07/c8012674-22cc-11e2-ac85-e669876c6a24_story.html.

27. "Record-Breaking Presidents Institute Explores Healthy Institutions and Strong Leadership," Council of Independent Colleges, January 7, 2020, https://www.cic.edu/news-information/independent-newsletter/PI-2020/presidents-institute.

28. "Liberal Arts," *Encyclopedia Britannica*, August 10, 2010, https://www.britannica.com/topic/liberal-arts.

29. Brandon Busteed, "Higher Education: Drop the Term Liberal Arts,'" Gallup, August 16, 2017, https://news.gallup.com/opinion/gallup/216275/higher-education-drop-term-liberal-arts.aspx.

30. Mariette Aborn, Ashley Finley, Kevin Miller, and Sean Ruddy, "Is College Worth the Time and Money? It Depends on Whom You Ask," American Association of Colleges and Universities and Bipartisan Policy Center, September 2021, https://dgmg81phhvh63.cloudfront.net/content/user-photos/Research/PDFs/BPC_Fed-State_Brief_R04.2.pdf.

31. Michael Greenstone and Adam Looney, "Regardless of the Cost, College Still Matters," Brookings, October 5, 2012, https://www.brookings.edu/blog/jobs/2012/10/05/regardless-of-the-cost-college-still-matters/.

32. Laura D'Andrea Tyson, "Getting More Bang for the Buck in Higher Education," *New York Times*, June 14, 2013, https://archive.nytimes.com/economix.blogs.nytimes.com/2013/06/14/getting-more-bang-for-the-buck-in-higher-education/?_r=0.

33. Earl Cheit, *The Useful Arts and the Liberal Tradition* (New York: McGraw-Hill, 1975), 3.

34. "Harvard College Curriculum, 1640–1880: Overview," Harvard University Archives, May 6, 2022, https://guides.library.harvard.edu/c.php?g=405381&p=6465805.

35. Cheit, *Useful Arts and the Liberal Tradition*, 9.

36. Laurence R. Veysey, *The Emergence of the American University* (Chicago: University of Chicago Press, 1965), 60.

37. Michael Bisesi, "Historical Developments in American Undergraduate Education: General Education and the Core Curriculum," *British Journal of Educational Studies* 30, no. 2 (1982): 199–212, https://doi.org/10.1080/00071005.1982.9973625.

38. Christopher Jencks and David Riesman, *The Academic Revolution* (Garden City, NY: Doubleday, 1968), 494.

39. Sarah Turner and John Bound, "Closing the Gap or Widening the Divide: The Effects of the G.I. Bill and World War II on the Educational Outcomes of Black Americans," *Journal of Economic History* 63, no. 1 (2003): 145–77, https://doi.org/10.1017/S0022050703001761.

40. R. L. Geiger, "The Ten Generations of American Higher Education," in M. N. Bastedo, P. A. Altbach, and P. J. Gumport, eds., *American Higher Education in the 21st Century: Social, Political, and Economic Challenges*, 4th ed. (Baltimore: Johns Hopkins University Press, 2016), 1–34.

41. Scott Carlson, "What's a College Degree Worth? The Imperfect Science and Contested Methods of Measuring the Return on Investment of College," *Chronicle*

of Higher Education, October 18, 2021, https://www.chronicle.com/article/whats-a-college-degree-worth?cid=gen_sign_in.

42. Michael Itzkowitz and Kylie Murdock, "Paying the Right Price for Your College Program," Third Way, October 19, 2021, https://www.thirdway.org/blog/paying-the-right-price-for-your-college-program.

43. Carlson, "What's a College Degree Worth?"

44. "Ranking 4,500 Colleges by ROI (2022)," Georgetown University Center on Education and the Workforce, February 15, 2022, https://cew.georgetown.edu/cew-reports/roi2022/.

45. Georgetown University Center on Education and the Workforce, "At 30% of Colleges, More Than Half of Students Earn Less Than High School Graduates after 10 Years, Georgetown CEW Finds," press release, February 15, 2022, https://1gyhoq479ufd3yna29x7ubjn-wpengine.netdna-ssl.com/wp-content/uploads/GeorgetownCEW_CollegeROI_PressRelease_2-15-22.pdf.

46. Stacy Berg Dale and Alan B. Krueger, "Estimating the Payoff to Attending a More Selective College: An Application of Selection on Observables and Unobservables," *Quarterly Journal of Economics* 117 no. 4 (2002): 1491–527, https://doi.org/10.1162/003355302320935089.

47. Stacy B. Dale and Alan B. Krueger, "Estimating the Effects of College Characteristics over the Career Using Administrative Earnings Data," *Journal of Human Resources* 49, no 2 (2014): 323–58, https://www.jstor.org/stable/23799087.

48. Matt Sigelman and Christopher B. Howard, "Dynamos for Diversity: How Higher Education Can Build a More Equitable Society," Burning Glass Institute, January 26, 2022, https://static1.squarespace.com/static/6197797102be715f55c0e0a1/t/61f047668e05e66170e99042/1643136870697/Dynamos+for+Diversity.FINAL.pdf.

49. Ibid.

50. Ibid.

51. Ibid.

52. Richard B. Freeman, *The Overeducated American* (New York: Academic, 1976).

53. David Autor, "Skills, Education, and the Rise of Earnings Inequality among the 'Other 99 Percent,'" *Science* 344 (2014), https://www.science.org/doi/10.1126/science.1251868.

54. Katherine Schaeffer, "10 Facts about Today's College Graduates," Pew Research Center, April 11, 2022, https://www.pewresearch.org/fact-tank/2022/04/12/10-facts-about-todays-college-graduates/.

55. Author interview with Susan Dynarski, Cambridge, MA, October 3, 2021.

56. Adam Looney, "Responses to Reader Questions about My Report 'Student Loan Forgiveness Is Regressive,'" Brookings, January 31, 2022, https://www.brookings.edu/blog/up-front/2022/01/31/responses-to-reader-questions-about-my-report-student-loan-forgiveness-is-regressive/.

57. Bryan Caplan, *The Case against Education: Why the Education System Is a Waste of Time and Money* (Princeton, NJ: Princeton University Press, 2019).

58. Author interview with Lawrence Katz, September 30, 2021.

59. Philip Oreopoulos, "Estimating Average and Local Average Treatment Effects of Education When Compulsory Schooling Laws Really Matter," *American Economic Review* 96, no. 2 (March, 2006): 152–75, https://www.jstor.org/stable/30034359.

60. Carolina Arteaga, "The Effect of Human Capital on Earnings: Evidence from a Reform at Colombia's Top University," *Journal of Public Economics* 157 (2018), https://doi.org/10.1016/j.jpubeco.2017.10.007.

61. Ibid., 212.

62. Kevin Carey, "Bad Job Market: Why the Media Is Always Wrong about the Value of a College Degree," *New Republic*, June 9, 2011, https://newrepublic.com/article/89675/bad-job-market-media-wrong-college-degree.

63. David Autor, Arindrajit Dube, and Annie McGrew, "The Unexpected Compression: Competition at Work in the Low Wage Labor Market," National Bureau of Economic Research Working Paper 31010, March 2023, http://www.nber.org/papers/w31010.

64. US Census Bureau, "Census Bureau Releases New Educational Attainment Data," press release, February 24, 2022, https://www.census.gov/newsroom/press-releases/2022/educational-attainment.html.

65. US Census Bureau, Current Population Survey, 2021 Annual Social and Economic Supplement, "Table 3. Detailed Years of School Completed by People 25 Years and over by Sex, Age Groups, Race and Hispanic Origin: 2021," https://www.census.gov/data/tables/2021/demo/educational-attainment/cps-detailed-tables.html, accessed February 7, 2023.

Chapter 3

1. Author interview with Jeffrey Diaz Vega, Washington, DC, December 3, 2021.

2. Ben Wildavsky and Aimée Eubanks Davis, "Gerald Chertavian," *Lessons Earned* podcast, Strada Education Network, March 17, 2021, https://stradaeducation.org/podcast/gerald-chertavian/.

3. Ibid.

4. "Our Approach," Year Up, https://www.yearup.org/.

5. Credential Engine (2022), "Counting U.S. Postsecondary and Secondary Credentials" (Washington, DC: Credential Engine), https://credentialengine.org /wp-content/uploads/2023/01/Final-CountingCredentials_2022.pdf.

6. "The Global Learner Survey," Pearson, September 2019, https://www.pearson .com/content/dam/global-store/global/resources/Pearson_Global_Learner _Survey_2019.pdf.

7. Paul Fain, "Alternative Credentials on the Rise," *Inside Higher Ed*, August 27, 2020, https://www.insidehighered.com/news/2020/08/27/interest-spikes-short -term-online-credentials-will-it-be-sustained.

8. Ibid.

9. Monique O. Ositelu, "Five Things Policymakers Should Know about Short-Term Credentials," New America, March 2, 2021, https://d1y8sb8igg2f8e .cloudfront.net/documents/Five_Things_Policymakers_Should_Know_About _Short-Term_Credentials.pdf.

10. Anthony P. Carnevale, "White Flight to the Bachelor's Degree," Georgetown University Center on Education and the Workforce, September 2, 2020, https:// medium.com/georgetown-cew/white-flight-to-the-ba-e604ee4e3967.

11. Ositelu, "Five Things Policymakers Should Know About Short-Term Credentials."

12. Monique O. Ositelu, Clare McCann, and Amy Laitinen, "The Short-Term Credentials Landscape," New America, May 3, 2021, https://www.newamerica.org /education-policy/reports/the-short-term-credentials-landscape/foreword-by -kevin-carey/.

13. Amy Laitinen quoted in Daniel C. Vock, "What Student Safeguards Are Needed If Congress Expands Pell to Short-Term Programs?," *Higher Ed Dive*, September 27, 2021, https://www.highereddive.com/news/what-student-safeguards -are-needed-if-congress-expands-pell-to-short-term-p/607221/.

14. Di Xu quoted in Erika B. Lewy, "Short-Term Training Programs Are Increasingly Popular, but Do They Work?" MDRC, February 2022, https://www.mdrc.org /publication/short-term-training-programs-are-increasingly-popular-do-they -work.

15. Howard S. Bloom, Larry L. Orr, Stephen H. Bell, George Cave, Fred Doolittle, Winston Lin, and Johannes M. Bos, "The Benefits and Costs of JTPA Title II-A Programs: Key Findings from the National Job Training Partnership Act Study," *Journal of Human Resources* 32, no. 3 (Summer, 1997): 549–76, http://

qe4policy.ec.unipi.it/wp-content/uploads/2015/09/The-Benefits-and-Costs-of
-JTPA.pdf.

16. Author interview with Garrett Warfield, Boston, October 5, 2021.

17. Samuel Lee and Caroline Garau, "Sectoral Employment Programs as a Path
to Quality Jobs: Lessons from Randomized Evaluations," Abdul Latif Jameel Poverty Action Lab, February 22, 2022, https://www.povertyactionlab.org/sites
/default/files/publication/Evidence-Review_Sectoral-Employment_2222022_0
.pdf.

18. L. F. Katz, J. Roth, R. Hendra, and K. Schaberg, "Why Do Sectoral Employment Programs Work? Lessons from Work Advance," *Journal of Labor Economics*
40, S1 (2022): S249–S291.

19. Lee and Garau, "Sectoral Employment Programs."

20. Author interview with Ryan Craig, video, March 18, 2022.

21. Credential Engine, "Counting U.S. Postsecondary and Secondary
Credentials."

22. Larry Good, Nan Travers, and Holly Zanville, "An Rx for an Ailing Postsecondary Education System: Credential as You Go," Corporation for a Skilled Workforce, November 24, 2020, https://corp4skilledwork.medium.com/an-rx-for-an
-ailing-postsecondary-education-system-credential-as-you-go-9a98071f440f.

23. Causey et al., "Some College, No Credential Student Outcomes, Annual
Progress Report—Academic Year 2020/21."

24. Author interview with Holly Zanville, video, March 14, 2022.

25. Liz Eggleston, "2020 Coding Bootcamp Alumni Outcomes & Demograph-
ics Report," Course Report, March 4, 2021, https://www.coursereport.com
/reports/2020-coding-bootcamp-alumni-outcomes-demographics-report
-during-covid-19.

26. Author interview with Sean Gallagher, Boston, October 5, 2021.

27. Laura Pappano, "The Year of the MOOC," *New York Times*, November 2,
2012, https://www.nytimes.com/2012/11/04/education/edlife/massive-open
-online-courses-are-multiplying-at-a-rapid-pace.html.

28. Andrew Hanson "Examining the Value of Nondegree Credentials," Strada
Center for Education Consumer Insights, July 28, 2021, https://cci.stradaeducation
.org/pv-release-july-28-2021/#.

29. Olivia Sanchez, "Trying to Give Students in Low-Wage Majors Some Extra
Skills They Can Cash In On," *Hechinger Report*, February 18, 2022, https://
hechingerreport.org/trying-to-give-students-in-low-wage-majors-some-extra
-skills-they-can-cash-in-on/?utm_medium=Social&utm_source=Facebook

&fbclid=IwAR32C_38DhAGkcGe0h1Dv84CgVS4jO9TugQ_s36-Vvex
HCTWYXhuCYrT0G4#Echobox=1649785021-1.

30. Hanson, "Examining the Value of Nondegree Credentials."

31. Jon Marcus, "Beer Making for Credit: Liberal Arts Colleges Add Career Tech," *Hechinger Report*, March 19, 2021, https://hechingerreport.org/some-academic-focused-colleges-are-adding-career-and-technical-training/.

32. Author interview with John Tebow, video, March 14, 2022.

33. Author interview with Terris Wallace, telephone, March 24, 2022.

34. Author interview with Terris Wallace, telephone, July 28, 2022.

35. Author interview with Tekla Moquin, video, February 16, 2022.

36. Allison Dulin Salisbury, "Building Equitable Upskilling Programs: It's Not Degree vs. Short Credentials—It's Both," *Forbes*, March 1, 2021, https://www.forbes.com/sites/allisondulinsalisbury/2021/03/01/building-equitable-upskilling-programs-its-not-degree-vs-short-credentials—its-both/?sh=3da998516079.

37. Thomas Bailey and Clive R. Bedfield, "Stackable Credentials: Do They Have Labor Market Value?," Community College Research Center of Teachers College, Columbia University, November 2017, https://ccrc.tc.columbia.edu/media/k2/attachments/stackable-credentials-do-they-have-labor-market-value.pdf.

38. "Student Success and Workforce Revitalization Task Force Report," Colorado Commission on Higher Education, December 2021, https://highered.colorado.gov/Publications/Reports/Legislative/1330/2021_SSWR_Task_Force_Report.pdf.

39. Matt Sigelman and Christopher B. Howard, "Dynamos for Diversity: How Higher Education Can Build a More Equitable Society," Burning Glass Institute, January 26, 2022, https://static1.squarespace.com/static/6197797102be715f55c0e0a1/t/61f047668e05e66170e99042/1643136870697/Dynamos+for+Diversity.FINAL.pdf.

Chapter 4

1. Author interview with Mark Granovetter, video, November 4, 2021.

2. Mark Granovetter, "The Strength of Weak Ties," *American Journal of Sociology* 78, no. 6 (1973), https://www.jstor.org/stable/2776392.

3. Philip S. DeOrtentiis, Chad H. Van Iddekinge, and Connie R. Wanberg, "Different Starting Lines, Different Finish Times: The Role of Social Class in the Job Search Process," *Journal of Applied Psychology*, May 17, 2021, http://dx.doi.org/10.1037/apl0000915.

4. Elaine W. Leigh, "Understanding Undergraduates' Career Preparation Experiences," Strada Center for Education Consumer Insights, December 8, 2021, https://cci.stradaeducation.org/pv-release-dec-8-2021/.

5. Ibid.

6. Author interview with Rachel Lipson, Washington, DC, December 13, 2021.

7. Author interview with Julia Freeland Fisher, Bethesda, MD, August 24, 2021.

8. Author interview with Garrett Warfield, Boston, October 5, 2021.

9. Julia Freeland Fisher, *Who You Know: Unlocking Innovations That Expand Students' Networks* (San Francisco: Jossey-Bass / Wiley, 2018), 9.

10. Ibid., 73.

11. Ibid., 74.

12. NapoleonCat, "Share of Facebook Users in the United States as of December 2022, by Age Group and Gender," Statista, January 9, 2023, https://www.statista.com/statistics/187549/facebook-distribution-of-users-age-group-usa/, accessed February 9, 2023.

13. Author interview with Meg Garlinghouse, San Francisco, November 12, 2021.

14. Karthik Rajkumar, Guillaume Saint-Jacques, Iavor Bojinov, Erik Brynjolfsson, and Sinan Aral, "A Causal Test of the Strength of Weak Ties," *Science* 377, no. 6612 (2022): 1304–10, https://doi.org/10.1126/science.abl4476.

15. Raj Chetty, Matthew O. Jackson, Theresa Kuchler, et al., "Social Capital I: Measurement and Associations with Economic Mobility," *Nature* 608 (2022): 108–21, https://doi.org/10.1038/s41586-022-04996-4.

16. Robert D. Putnam, *Bowling Alone: The Collapse and Revival of American Community* (New York: Touchstone, 2000).

17. Amanda Mull, "The Pandemic Has Erased Entire Categories of Friendship," *Atlantic*, January 27, 2021, https://www.theatlantic.com/health/archive/2021/01/pandemic-goodbye-casual-friends/617839/.

18. Meg Garlinghouse, "Closing the Network Gap," *LinkedIn Official Blog*, September 26, 2019, https://blog.linkedin.com/2019/september/26/closing-the-network-gap.

19. Jon Marcus, "College Degree Doesn't Pay Off as Well for First-Generation Grads," *Hechinger Report*, September 24, 2021, https://hechingerreport.org/college-degree-doesnt-pay-off-as-well-for-first-generation-grads/.

20. "Beyond Skills: How Social Capital Creates Economic Opportunity," SkillUp, Climb Hire, and Common Group, May 2021, 6, https://www.commongroup.org/wp-content/uploads/2021/12/BeyondSkills-HowSocialCapitalCreatesEconomicOpportunity.pdf.

21. Dana Hamdan, "Career Readiness in the COVID World," *Inside Higher Ed*, February 5, 2021, https://www.insidehighered.com/views/2021/02/05/wake-pandemic-and-racial-protests-colleges-must-transform-their-career-services.

22. Handshake, Home (LinkedIn page), LinkedIn, https://www.linkedin.com/company/team-handshake/, accessed February 9, 2023.

23. Natalia Garcia, personal email communication to author, January 28, 2022.

24. Author interview with Christine Cruzvergara, video, January 10, 2022.

25. Author interview with Alexandra Bernadotte, Oakland, CA, November 11, 2021.

26. Author interview with Michelle Dew, Oakland, CA, November 10, 2021.

27. See Braven, https://bebraven.org/, accessed February 9, 2023.

28. Author interview with Andrej Gjorgiev, Newark, NJ, November 15, 2021.

29. Ben Wildavsky and Andrew Hanson, "Aimée Eubanks Davis," *Lessons Earned* podcast, Strada Education Network, May 7, 2020, https://stradaeducation.org/podcast/episode-3-aimee-eubanks-davis/.

30. Ashley Arocho and Kasia Kalata, "Braven Launches at the City College of New York," press release, September 7, 2022, https://bebraven.org/braven-launches-at-the-city-college-of-new-york/.

31. Kasia Kalata and Joe King, "Braven Partners with Northern Illinois University with Fully Virtual Programming," press release, September 7, 2022, https://bebraven.org/bravenpartnerswithniu/.

32. Author interview with Farzana Chowdhury, video, November 17, 2021.

33. Author video interview with Markus Ward, October 14, 2021.

34. Author interview with Kalani Leifer, San Francisco, November 11, 2021.

35. Author interview with Nitzan Pelman, Berkeley, CA, November 10, 2021.

36. I'm grateful to Julia Freeland Fisher for underscoring this point.

37. Garlinghouse, "Closing the Network Gap."

Chapter 5

1. "About Accelerate ED," Accelerate ED, https://www.accelerate-ed.org/about, accessed February 9, 2023.

2. Author interview with Anthony P. Carnevale, video, August 27, 2021.

3. "Undergraduate Degree Fields," National Center for Education Statistics, May 2022, https://nces.ed.gov/programs/coe/indicator/cta/undergrad-degree-fields#suggested-citation.

4. "Bachelor's Degrees Conferred by Postsecondary Institutions, by Field of Study: Selected Years, 1970–71 through 2019–20," National Center for Education Statistics, January 2021, https://nces.ed.gov/programs/digest/d21/tables/dt21_322.10.asp.

5. Ibid.

6. Ibid. National Center for Education Statistics data show 7.2 percent of bachelor's degrees are conferred in "Engineering and Engineering Technologies." The latter category includes engineering-related fields such as construction trades and mechanic and repair technologies.

7. Jeffrey J. Selingo, "Business Is the Most Popular College Major, but That Doesn't Mean It's a Good Choice," *Washington Post*, January 28, 2017, https://www.washingtonpost.com/news/grade-point/wp/2017/01/28/business-is-the-most-popular-college-major-but-that-doesnt-mean-its-a-good-choice/.

8. "Community College FAQs—Community College Enrollment and Completion," Community College Research Center, Teachers College, Columbia University, 2021, https://ccrc.tc.columbia.edu/community-college-faqs.html.

9. Maria S. Cormier, Thomas Brock, James Jacobs, Richard Kazis, and Hayley Glatter, "Preparing for Tomorrow's Middle-Skill Jobs: How Community Colleges Are Responding to Technology Innovation in the Workplace," Community College Research Center, Teachers College, Columbia University, April 2022, https://ccrc.tc.columbia.edu/publications/tomorrows-middle-skill-jobs-community-colleges.html.

10. Paul Fain, "Even Some College Tends to Pay Off," *Inside Higher Ed*, August 22, 2019, https://www.insidehighered.com/news/2019/08/22/students-some-college-and-no-credential-still-benefit-labor-market.

11. Georgia Tech president G. Wayne Clough quoted in Thomas L. Friedman, *The World Is Flat: A Brief History of the Twenty-First Century* (New York: Farrar, Straus and Giroux, 2005), 324.

12. Michael J. Weiss and Howard S. Bloom, "'What Works' for Community College Students?," MDRC, June 2022, https://www.mdrc.org/sites/default/files/THE-RCT_Synthesis_Brief.pdf.

13. Michelle R. Weise, Andrew R. Hanson, and Yustina Saleh, "The New Geography of Skills: Regional Skill Shapes for the New Learning Ecosystem," Strada Institute for the Future of Work, December 2019, http://www.economicmodeling.com/wp-content/uploads/2020/01/NewGeographyOfSkills_Final_0109 2020.pdf.

14. Ben Wildavsky, "Anant Agarwal on MOOCs, Microcredentials, and the Democratization of Higher Education," *Higher Ed Spotlight* podcast, October 11, 2022, https://podcasts.apple.com/us/podcast/anant-agarwal-on-moocs-micro credentials-and/id1620239101?i=1000582255523.

15. Author interview with Sarah Turner, video, September 10, 2021.

16. Kerry Fulcher, "Reinvent Career Services to Create Pathways to Employ-ability," *Inside Higher Ed*, June 21, 2022, https://www.insidehighered.com/views /2022/06/21/structural-changes-help-embed-career-prep-academic-work -opinion.

17. Jon Marcus, "With Enrollment Sliding, Liberal Arts Colleges Struggle to Make a Case for Themselves," *Hechinger Report*, May 18, 2018, https://hechinger report.org/with-enrollment-sliding-liberal-arts-colleges-struggle-to-make-a-case -for-themselves/.

18. Ibid.

19. Michelle R. Weise, *Long Life Learning: Preparing for Jobs that Don't Even Exist Yet* (Hoboken, NJ: John Wiley and Sons, 2020).

20. Eric Rosenbaum, "Amazon, Walmart, Target Are Paying for College, but Money Isn't Everything in Education," *CNBC Workforce Wire*, September 28, 2021, https://www.cnbc.com/2021/09/28/the-boom-in-low-wage-worker-free college -is-about-to-get-tested.html.

21. Author interview with Ardine Williams, video, August 31, 2021.

22. Aimée Eubanks Davis, "How to Build Your Network as a First-Generation Student," *Ascend—Harvard Business Review*, February 15, 2022, https://hbr.org /2022/02/how-to-build-your-network-as-a-first-generation-student.

23. Julia Freeland Fisher and Mahnaz Charania, "5 Steps for Building & Strengthening Students' Networks," Christensen Institute, May 5, 2021, https:// whoyouknow.org/wp-content/uploads/2021/05/playbook2.pdf.

24. Ibid., 9.

25. Ben Wildavsky, "How to Fix the College to Career Pipeline—Christine Cruzvergara," *Higher Ed Spotlight* podcast, August 2, 2022, https://podcasts.apple .com/us/podcast/how-to-fix-the-college-to-career-pipeline/id1620239101?i=100 0574748343.

26. Ellen Sherberg, "In Her Own Words: Nolvia Delgado's Women's Network Worked for Her," *Bizwomen: The Business Journals*, May 5, 2022, https://www .bizjournals.com/bizwomen/news/latest-news/2022/05/in-her-own-words -novia-delgado.html?page=all.

27. Author interview with David Deming, Cambridge, MA, October 5, 2021.

28. Anthony P. Carnevale, Jeff Strohl, Nicole Smith, Ban Cheah, Artem Gulish, and Kathryn Peltier Campbell, "Navigating the College-to-Career Pathway," Georgetown University Center on Education and the Workforce, May 2021, https://files.eric.ed.gov/fulltext/ED617093.pdf.

29. Ben Wildavsky and Anna Gatlin Schilling, "Van Ton-Quinlivan," *Lessons Earned* podcast, Strada Education Network, March 2, 2020, https://stradaeducation.org/podcast/episode-6-van-ton-quinlivan/.

Index